Undoing Conquest

Undoing Conquest

Ancient Israel, the Bible, and the Future of Christianity

Kate Common

ORBIS BOOKS
Maryknoll, New York 10545

Founded in 1970, Orbis Books endeavors to publish works that enlighten the mind, nourish the spirit, and challenge the conscience. The publishing arm of the Maryknoll Fathers and Brothers, Orbis seeks to explore the global dimensions of the Christian faith and mission, to invite dialogue with diverse cultures and religious traditions, and to serve the cause of reconciliation and peace. The books published reflect the views of their authors and do not represent the official position of the Maryknoll Society. To learn more about Maryknoll and Orbis Books, please visit our website at www.orbisbooks.com.

Library of Congress Cataloging-in-Publication Data

Names: Common, Kate, author.
Title: Undoing conquest : ancient Israel, the Bible, an the future of Christianity / Kate Common.
Description: Maryknoll, NY : Orbis Books, [2024] | Includes bibliographical references and index. | Summary: "Explores the conquest narrative in the Book of Joshua"—Provided by publisher.
Identifiers: LCCN 2023036626 (print) | LCCN 2023036627 (ebook) | ISBN 9781626985582 | ISBN 9798888660164 (epub)
Subjects: LCSH: Violence in the Bible. | Bible. Old Testament—Social scientific criticism. | Sociology, Biblical. | Jews—History—1200-953 B.C. | Violence—Religious aspects—Christianity. | Church year.
Classification: LCC BS1199.V56 C66 2024 (print) | LCC BS1199.V56 (ebook) | DDC 221.6—dc23/eng/20231024
LC record available at https://lccn.loc.gov/2023036626
LC ebook record available at https://lccn.loc.gov/2023036627

Dedicated to the Hebrew Highland Settlers,
whose story crosses millennia and keeps me writing

Contents

Acknowledgements

This book has taken a village.

Foremost, I gratefully acknowledge Mary Elizabeth Moore, who believed in this project when others did not, encouraged me to keep going, and helped me cultivate the skills I needed to write it. I am forever indebted to your careful listening, curious questions, and guiding insights throughout all of our work together. You have shaped me into the teacher and scholar I am today.

Thank you, Kathe Pfister Darr and Brandon J. Simonson, my biblical studies interlocutors. Kathe taught me the beginnings of ancient Hebrew, listened carefully to my ideas, guided my reading, and offered key feedback on my biblical studies chapters. Brandon's energy and ideas inspired me to hone my biblical studies research and to imagine new interdisciplinary Highland Settlements scholarship. I am grateful for the mentorship of Teddy Hickman-Maynard, who highlighted the importance of this project for the church and whose vital encouragement kept me going as challenges arose.

I am grateful for Susan Schnur, a key emotional and editorial midwife to the project. Thanks for all of your support, for reading an early draft, and for providing your editorial feedback. The book is better for it. I am appreciative of the editorial work of Cade Jerrell, who carefully read and edited earlier drafts. I have much gratitude and thanks to Thomas

Hermans-Webster, for his editorial support, excitement for the
project, and seeing the importance of the work in connection
with *The Tribes of Yahweh*. I could not be more grateful for
Tom's editorial suggestions and polishes. I am also grateful
to Orbis Books for seeing the importance of the project especially in connection to the classic text *The Tribes of Yahweh*.
I am honored.

Thank you to the Louisville Institute and Methodist Theological School in Ohio for the opportunity these past years to
develop as an educator and scholar. It was not easy to finish
a PhD in a global pandemic and their support made the next
phases of my career possible. Thanks Ian White Maher for
seeing the significance of *Undoing Conquest* for churches and
ministers. I am grateful for Ian's support and for the Seek-
ers Table online platform to bring these ideas forward into a
public theology course. A special thanks to my mom, Karen
Common, who has listened over the phone to many drafts and
discussions on the topic. I appreciate her willingness to always
help me mull over an idea or paragraph. And, of course, I am
ever grateful for the grounding presence of my spouse, Kysa
Nygreen. It is easy to do hard things with your support.

Lastly, I am grateful for the many archeologists and biblical
scholars over the decades who have unearthed the Highland
Settlements story. Especially to Norman K. Gottwald, who
saw the connection between the Highland Settlers story and
social justice now, thank you. It is my honor to continue working through these ideas in his shadow.

Introduction

The stories we tell shape our identities, who we are as a people, and what we come to expect in the world. Stories told together hold us together, shaping our collective or social imagination.[1] Our religious traditions contain many stories that shape us. Around the world, the stories of the Hebrew people have become foundational for the biblical faith traditions. Their stories are canonized in the Bible, which many people hold as sacred text, even the word of God. So what do we do when we begin to realize that some biblical stories contribute to actual violence in the world? What do we do when our stories are harmful and no longer serve us? This book explores one such story, the conquest narrative found in the book of Joshua in the Hebrew Bible (Josh 1–11).

The conquest narrative is a story that justifies patterns and practices of colonialism, land-taking, and even genocide in religious imagination.[2] The story has enabled violent atrocities to be understood in the minds of primarily Christian perpetra-

---

[1]Charles Taylor's description of the social imaginary is the space inhabited with myths, symbols, and stories, which create the norms of the social space. Charles Taylor, *Modern Social Imaginaries*, Public Planet Books (Durham, NC: Duke University Press, 2004), 23.

[2]Willie James Jennings names the European colonial and racist Christian imagination "diseased." See Willie James Jennings, *The Christian Imagination: Theology and the Origins of Race* (New Haven, CT: Yale University Press, 2010), 6.

tors as not only justified but divinely sanctioned. The European genocide of Indigenous Peoples across the Americas and the apartheid state in South Africa are a few of the historical atrocities supported by the conquest narrative in colonial religious imagination. There are no land or peoples safe when any land can become the promised land and any people the Canaanites. These horrors do not remain in the past. They are part of our present, in large part because an imagination of conquest remains. But what do we do about a story so thoroughly embedded and entangled in the dominant faith, culture, and Western social imagination? How do we *undo conquest*? We cannot undo the past, but we must work toward undoing the legacies of conquest within our own communities.

Because stories affect identity, part of social justice work must be to reshape violent historical stories that contribute to harmful and even genocidal social imaginaries. Without doing so, these stories lie dormant as hidden inheritances that are carried forward into an unknown future, where they can once again be used to foster and perpetrate violence.[3] The past is never in the past.

The good news is that the stories we tell can and do change. Religious traditions themselves are living communities, constantly on the dialogical move. Unlike static entities, they perennially negotiate the tensions between past and present, reshaping and reimaging stories in order to meet the current moment. The process can seem slow and even imperceptible, but change is occurring. New stories, new theologies, new practices, new images of the Divine develop as human cultures morph and change. Indeed, change is necessary as stasis leads to death. The task of undoing conquest, then, is consistent with processes inherent to religious traditions rather than a unique

---

[3]Mary McClintock Fulkerson, *Places of Redemption: Theology for a Worldly Church* (Oxford: Oxford University Press, 2010), 11.

problem. Even when stories are part of sacred texts, in this case the Bible, they are constantly up for new interpretation and new ways of understanding. New interpretations of old stories and even new histories are important for social change. When new meaning is made from the past, new beginnings occur.[4]

Feminist and other critical theorists contend that the key to the future is found in the past: how we perceive the past informs the way we shape our present, which, in turn, shapes the future.[5] Disrupting the past and reimagining it can "disrupt the certainties of the present and so [open] the way to imagining a different future."[6] History is a site of the political. In some cases, new information or discoveries are made that shed new light on our oldest stories and histories and press for a new interpretation. Sometimes, such a historical discovery can unsettle the very foundation of history.

Newly Discovered History of Ancient Israel

During the past century, archaeologists made such a finding when they unearthed a new history of the origins of the

---

[4]Rebecca S. Chopp, "Christian Moral Imagination: A Feminist Practical Theology and the Future of Theological Education," *International Journal of Practical Theology* 1, no. 1 (January 1, 1997): 106.

[5]Rosemary Radford Ruether, *Gaia & God: An Ecofeminist Theology of Earth Healing* (San Francisco: HarperCollins, 1994); Elisabeth Schüssler Fiorenza, *In Memory of Her: A Feminist Theological Reconstruction of Christian Origins*, 10th ann. ed. (New York: Crossroad, 1994); Riane Eisler, *The Chalice and the Blade: Our History, Our Future* (San Francisco: Harper-Collins, 1988); Gerda Lerner, *The Creation of Patriarchy* (New York: Oxford University Press, 1986).

[6]Elaine Graham, "A Remembrance of Things (Best) Forgotten: The 'Allegorical Past' and the Feminist Imagination," *Feminist Theology* 21, no. 1 (2012): 65. Here Graham quotes directly from feminist Joan Scott.

Hebrew people in Canaan (present-day Israel and Palestine), known as the Iron Age I Hebrew Highland Settlements.[7] Archaeologists discovered and excavated hundreds of small villages, found scattered across the highland regions of ancient Canaan that date to the end of the Late Bronze Age and into the early Iron Age. Carefully excavated artifacts, like shards of pottery and layers of stones, now provide the foundation for a new history of the ancient Hebrew people in Canaan— a history that counters the story of conquest. Archaeological evidence indicates that the social process that led to the origins of the Hebrew people was not a violent military overtaking as the Bible depicts in the book of Joshua. Rather, the Hebrew people emerged in Canaan in a nonmilitaristic social response to extreme social and climate conditions.

During this tumultuous period in Canaan, people faced severe drought, oppressive socioeconomic conditions, and the collapse of the Egyptian Empire. In response to these co-alescing dynamics, groups of largely indigenous Canaanites carved out a new way of life in the geographically remote and rocky hillsides of the Canaan highlands. Though the settlements were in close proximity to Egyptian-controlled land, the rocky terrain kept them insulated from Egyptian military control. Horses and chariots could not navigate the difficult, rocky terrain. The lack of military intervention enabled the

---

[7]I choose to capitalize "Highland Settlements" throughout this book as a literary means to indicate the sacredness of their story even though it resides outside the pages of the Bible. Because the Highland Settlements represent the origins of the Hebrew people and are considered proto-Israelite, I am honoring them within this lineage by choosing to capitalize the references to this community even if this is not always the practice within archaeological and biblical studies research. I would like to thank Dr. Susan Schnur for this suggestion along with her feedback on an earlier draft.

Highland Settlements to expand for a nearly 150-year period.[8] During this time, these new settlements appeared to idealize, if not practice, a type of heterarchical or even egalitarian social organization, likely in response to the harsh and unjust conditions they left under Egyptian imperial rule. The Hebrew and, later, Israelite identity developed through a process of ethnogenesis as Canaanite settlers began to shape a new culture through their innovative social, language, farming, and cultic practices.[9]

The biblical story of the Israelite conquest of Canaan covers over the Highland Settlement period of Israelite history. Unearthing this buried history once again is an archaeological miracle of sorts. Because Israelite history is a foundational historical narrative for Western cultures, new historical developments concerning Israelite origins, like the discovery of the Highland Settlements, can have a wide impact across different cultural and religious spheres.

Archaeological evidence from the Iron Age may not be readily understood as an inspirational source for contemporary Christian imagination. Inspiration from the Iron Age? Really? While this is an understandable reaction, because Christianity is shaped by the historical narratives contained in Hebrew Scriptures, new discoveries about the history of the Hebrew people can have an important bearing on Christian theology, even histories from the Iron Age.

---

[8] A few biblical scholars disagree with such an interpretation of the archaeological evidence. For one primary example of biblical scholars who argue for the likely historicity of the conquest narrative as is told in the biblical narrative, see Iain W. Provan, V. Philips Long, and Tremper Longman, *A Biblical History of Israel*, 2nd ed. (Louisville, KY: Westminster John Knox, 2015).

[9] For discussion on the ethnogenesis of Israelite identity, see Avraham Faust, *Israel's Ethnogenesis: Settlement, Interaction, Expansion and Resistance*, Approaches to Anthropological Archaeology (London: Equinox, 2006).

Many people are familiar with the biblical stories of Hebrew origins, like Abraham migrating to Canaan (Genesis 12–26); the exodus from Egypt (Exodus 1–15), and the Israelite conquest of the promised land (Joshua 1–11). However, few people outside of specialized academic fields like archaeology, biblical studies, and ancient Near Eastern studies know of the archaeological evidence surrounding Hebrew origins. Yet the Highland Settlements archaeological evidence is too important to remain only within specialized academic audiences because it provides fresh perspectives on the origins of the Hebrew tradition, with the potential to reshape social imagination.

Challenge to Biblical Authority

The discovery of the Highland Settlements can challenge how people understand the Bible, and the settlements' information can bring to the fore issues about biblical authority and the historical-critical contexts of certain biblical texts like the book of Joshua, and even Judges and Exodus. The biblical conquest story and the archaeological evidence of Israelite origins in Canaan do not only differ—they contradict one another. These differences inherently raise questions about the historical accuracy of the Bible that many people hold as sacred text: How do we understand the origins of Israel with this discrepancy in mind?

People who take for granted that the Bible, while not factually inerrant, can be trusted to allude to actual historical events can find it upending to learn that the conquest narrative creates an alternative history of Hebrew origins in Canaan. Furthermore, the narrative was likely fabricated hundreds of years later to support specific geopolitical claims—fake news, so to speak. This information can be downright upsetting, and it could possibly be outright rejected by those who hold the Bible as historically accurate and factually inerrant. If the conquest is not true, what else might not be? I relate to this challenge since my earliest Christian communities taught me to read the Bible as inerrant and literal. For me it was a lengthy process to reconcile the idea that not all of what you read in the Bible may be literally true, yet the Bible can still be an authoritative sacred text.

The upside to the challenge is that the Highland Settlements' information presents a didactic opening to invite deeper study and analysis of the biblical texts. The book discusses what biblical scholarship reveals about the conquest narrative and why it was written. It also examines how different Christian approaches to violent biblical texts like the conquest narrative, may not be enough to deal with legacies of violence that such texts have supported. *Undoing Conquest* dives into biblical scholarship, questions of biblical authority, hermeneutic approaches, and deeper understandings of the Bible itself. For those who love and revere the Bible, these topics can deepen knowledge and appreciation of the good book, including violent texts like the conquest narrative. In short, for some people, this study can enhance biblical literacy.

I recognize that there are schools of religious scholarship and religious devotion that conceive of the Bible as sacred text in such a way that this project will appear offensive. While I respect such a position, it does not reflect my own approach. I hold a view of the Bible as sacred text that is not dependent upon it being historically accurate. I write within a tradition that upholds that there can be beauty and appreciation of the text found in these nuances. I offer an example of how new information can be intentionally integrated into Christian imagination and praxis.

Appropriating Conquest

At the outset of the project, I find it necessary to underscore that the problem with the conquest narrative in Joshua is not the biblical story itself but, rather, in how imperial Christians appropriated Israelite history. It is essential to make this distinction because Christians can easily discredit the Israelite conquest narrative as "bad" history. This easy dismissal from a Christian perspective can replicate an anti-Semitic, supersessionist theology that stereotypes the Hebrew Bible as containing a violent, vengeful image of God in contrast to viewing the New Testament texts as revealing a loving and just God.[10] Because *Undoing Conquest* engages directly with the conquest narrative found in the Hebrew texts, I am wary of replicating this supersessionist tendency by simply critiquing the conquest narrative as the problem—such an interpretive strategy inherently places blame on the texts themselves. While violent texts in the Bible present hermeneutical challenges, easily dismissing them is not an apt answer. More interpretive nuance is needed.

A historical-critical interpretive approach examines the sociopolitical context from which the conquest narrative was written. This research provides greater clarity as to why the biblical history of Israel includes a violent story of conquest and not a story of a peaceful settlement process. Biblical studies research shows that the conquest story was first written around 600 BCE, in Judah, from people traumatized and

---

[10]Salvation history or *Heilsgeschichte* (the German name) is a theological perspective that divides the Hebrew Bible from the New Testament or interprets Jesus as a new revelation that supersedes the prior Israelite tradition.

terrorized by the Assyrian Empire for centuries. A trauma-informed perspective shows that Judeans on the margins of empire sought to craft their history in a way that mirrored the empires surrounding them to empower themselves.[11] Taken in the context of Assyrian terror and trauma, the themes of the conquest story are understandable. Ironically, in the hands of Christian empires and imperial churches, the conquest story from 600 BCE became a tool in the arsenal of Christian colonialism and genocide.

Gottwald's The Tribes of Yahweh

In his classic book *The Tribes of Yahweh*, Norman Gottwald hypothesized that ancient Israel emerged from a "peasant counterculture resisting state control."[12] Gottwald saw the potential for the Highland Settlements to inspire justice because he made a connection between social justice movements seeking to make a better society and the Highland Settlements that were based on utopic societal ideals.[13] What is important

---

[11]David M. Carr, *Holy Resilience: The Bible's Traumatic Origins* (New Haven, CT: Yale University Press, 2014).

[12]Norman K. Gottwald, "Political Activism and Biblical Scholarship: An Interview," in *Tracking* The Tribes of Yahweh*: On the Trail of a Classic*, ed. Roland Boer (London: Sheffield Academic, 2002), 163; Norman K. Gottwald, *The Tribes of Yahweh: A Sociology of the Religion of Liberated Israel, 1250–1050 B.C.E.* (Maryknoll, NY: Orbis, 1979). Gottwald applied a Marxist sociological perspective to develop his interpretation. *Tribes* prompted much dialogue, analysis, and critique across biblical studies. Despite this critique, many details of Gottwald's initial hypothesis remain central to Highland Settlements interpretation today.

[13]Gottwald made this connection during the 1960s while working on the book in Berkeley, California, and witnessing social justice movements of the time. Gottwald, "Political Activism and Biblical Scholarship," 163.

here is that the Highland Settlements are not a "rootless uto-pia," but form a history that is firmly lodged in the memory of the three major biblical traditions.[14] *The Tribes of Yahweh* encouraged "Christians and Jews to reclaim biblical tradition as a relevant resource for their own hopes and endeavors for positive social change."[15]

Tribes influenced a broad array of communities, from aca-demic biblical studies to churches and synagogues. Political prisoners in South Africa passed *Tribes* around from cell to cell and considered it a holy book; Latin American nuns cre-ated flip charts of Highland Settlements material to inspire their base communities; a Korean biblical scholar who was imprisoned as a political dissident had a copy of *Tribes* that he began to understand in prison.[16] The influence of *Tribes* confirms that the Highland Settlements can make "a practi-cal, life-sustaining difference in religious and para-religious communities."[17]

Despite the influence of *The Tribes of Yahweh*, many people still do not know about the Highland Settlements. While much has been written across biblical and archaeological studies, the Highland Settlements story remains largely out of reach for people without access to specialized discourse. The Highland

---

[14]Gottwald, "Response to Contributors," in *Tracking* The Tribes of Yah-weh, 182–84.

[15]Norman K. Gottwald, "Revisiting *The Tribes of Yahweh*," *Servicios Koinonia: Servicio Biblico Latinoamericano* 374; Gottwald, "Response to Contributors," 181.

[16]Gottwald, "Response to Contributors," 181; Gottwald, "Political Activism and Biblical Scholarship: An Interview," 166–67. Gottwald notes that the book has influenced political activists in the United States, Korea, the Philippines, South Africa, and Latin America. These are just the people from whom he received correspondence.

[17]Gottwald, "Response to Contributors," 181.

Settlements story has yet to be incorporated into the life of the church and other faith communities in any substantial way. Gottwald discussed the necessity for theological interpretation and asked how theologians can connect the early Israelite historical evidence with communities seeking "justice here and now."[18] Theologians still need to grapple with the meaning of the Highland Settlements in connection to the construction of theology and religious practices. *Undoing Conquest* begins this work.

Theological Reflection

The lack of theological reflection seeking to integrate the Highland Settlements story into religious practice reflects a typical pattern of cultural integration of profound discoveries, according to Thomas Kuhn's studies of scientific paradigm shifts. Kuhn found that new discoveries can take around one hundred years to be incorporated.[19] With this pattern in mind, it has been nearly a century since the first Highland Settlements discoveries were made. Now is the time to integrate the settlements discovery more fully into the life of biblical faith communities and into wider culture. Such a discovery is too important to remain unintegrated into religious life and praxis.

Undoing Conquest begins the work of theological reflection on the Highland Settlements research from a feminist theologi-

---

[18]Gottwald, "Response to Contributors," 184. As a biblical scholar, Gottwald did not do the needed theological interpretation. He does not mention theologians explicitly in his article, but it seems implied since this type of interpretive work is the task of practical theologians.

[19]Thomas Kuhn, *The Structure of Scientific Revolutions* (Chicago: University of Chicago Press, 1962).

cal standpoint, with a focus on interpreting the meaning of the settlements for Christian practice today. This book argues that the Highland Settlements material can be interpreted as a liberating counterhistory that can challenge the imagination of conquest and prompt new Christian imagination and praxis for churches today. Counterhistories typically read against the grain of dominant histories and challenge dominant forms of knowledge and power.[20] Since the Highland Settlements story has been largely lost due to the biblical story of conquest, it can be considered a counterhistory. As a counterhistory to conquest, the Highland Settlements research can challenge the problematic ways the Joshua conquest story has shaped what Willie James Jennings calls a diseased Christian social imagination.[21] Simply put, the Highland Settlements can be understood as a counterhistory from the ancient past that can help prompt liberative imagination today.[22]

---

[20]WordSense.eu, s.v. "counterhistory." Elaine Graham explains that counter-histories can inspire new social imagination because "It is necessary to 'read against the grain' of history in order to redeem it; whether it be through the telling and retelling of how we got where we are, or painstaking scholarship [to] excavate the stories of our foremothers, or the writing of fantastical science fiction as both inspiration and warning. All such genres are 'sketches toward a counterhistory' (Jantzen, 1994: 188) in which agency, power and knowledge are radically re-envizaged." Graham, "A Remembrance of Things (Best) Forgotten," 12. Additionally, Emilie M. Townes writes about "countermemories," which is similar to the concept of counterhistory. Townes discusses the power of countermemory in the context of the United States: "Countermemory has the potential to challenge the false generalizations and gross stereotypes often found in what passes for 'history' in the United States." Emilie M. Townes, *Womanist Ethics and the Cultural Production of Evil* (New York: Palgrave Macmillan, 2006), 47.

[21]Jennings, *The Christian Imagination*, 6.

[22]Emilie M. Townes discusses the power of countermemories to challenge dominant generalizing and stereotyping histories. Townes, *Womanist Ethics and the Cultural Production of Evil*, 45–48.

Undoing Conquest

The title *Undoing Conquest* nods toward the gender studies concept exemplified in Judith Butler's text *Undoing Gender*: gender is a social construction and, as such, can be undone.[23] Socially constructed things still have real-world consequences. Understanding the socially constructed nature of a thing can open avenues to choose to do a thing otherwise. The Highland Settlements archaeological evidence provides a contrasting history to conquest and, by doing so, reveals the constructive nature of the conquest narrative in the book of Joshua. Upholding the Highland Settlements as a counterhistory to conquest can bring about liberative and justice-oriented real-world consequences.

Churches often examine their current praxis, seeking transformation in moments of change and decline. Such processes of change typically involve examining the past to reconstitute the present. *Undoing Conquest* challenges churches to seek to undo conquest within Christian imagination and praxis by examining the past. To undo conquest, churches that bear the legacies of colonial violence will need to take responsibility for the conquests in the history of Christianity. Such churches will need to seek reconciliation and reparations for those still living in the traumatic wake of these conquests. They must actively seek to decolonize the church's theology and praxis. One decolonial practice is to loosen or unfasten the image of conquest as the predominant story of Hebrew origins from the Christian imagination.[24]

---

[23]Judith P. Butler, *Gender Trouble* (New York: Routledge, 1999); Judith P. Butler, *Undoing Gender* (New York: Routledge, 2004).

[24]Here, I draw on the definition of undoing as the act of unfastening or loosening. Merriam-Webster.com, s.v. "undoing."

Not all churches fall into these categories. Predominantly Indigenous Peoples' churches, Black churches, and immigrant churches, for example, do not have the same decolonizing and reparative tasks ahead of them. Their task may be toward the continued healing of historic and contemporary traumas inflicted by the conquests of colonial powers and churches. For such people and churches, the Highland Settlements offer a liberative story of Hebrew origins that aligns with stories of the oppressed and not of the empire.

Undoing Conquest introduces the Highland Settlements story and suggests ways to integrate the story into the practice of churches that considers churches both with colonial legacies and those on the margins of colonial power. To undo conquest, all churches share the task of intentionally reshaping Christian imagination in ways that can counter the imagination of conquest now and in the future. These are some of the ways that this book seeks to undo conquest.

These tasks are not easy. So, in the latter part of the book, I suggest a new liturgical season that can provide a yearly space for churches to dedicate to this work—what I call the "Season of Origins." The work of undoing conquest cannot be accomplished quickly. It will require an annual return to build new practices and theologies cumulatively. Given the profundity of the Highland Settlements discovery and the horrific ways that Christians have leveraged the conquest history as their own, a practice as encompassing as a new liturgical season is appropriate to deal with histories of conquest within Christianity.

Audience

Undoing Conquest invites deeper engagement with topics of Israelite history, the Bible, and new imagination for liberative church praxis. It encourages people to learn about violent Christian histories, to interrupt problematic patterns, and to reconcile and heal from the past. The book is a practical theological text that does interdisciplinary work engaging the Bible, biblical scholarship, and archaeological research. Such interdisciplinary work has been largely missing in practical theology.[25] I hope that scholars in practical theology and biblical studies will be among its readers. *Undoing Conquest* can be used in a theological school classroom, particularly in courses focused on biblical study, practical theology, or the theological imagination, to name a few. I have also written the book with churches and religious leaders in mind, especially those who are leading and imagining new ways of building community as a response to ecological, decolonial, and social pressures. I encourage churches and other faith communities to form reading groups to read and discuss it together. Likewise, anyone interested in how history shapes the present will find this book useful, especially as the United States is embroiled in controversies of what history gets to be told in public education. I hope that *Undoing Conquest* will prompt theological reflection and new praxis across a variety of contexts.

Chapter Summary

Chapter 1 considers the importance of the Highland Settlements for theology as it may not be readily obvious how Iron Age I archaeological evidence is relevant today. The chapter

---

[25]Margaret Whipp, Paul H. Ballard, Christopher Rowland, and Zoë Bennett offer a few examples of practical theology texts that discuss using the Bible in practical theology. Margaret Whipp, "Lucky Lections: On Using the Bible in Practical Theology," *Practical Theology* 5, no. 3 (December 1, 2012): 341–44; Paul H. Ballard, "The Bible in Theological Reflection: Indications from the History of Scripture," *Practical Theology* 4, no. 1 (April 1, 2011): 35–47; Christopher Rowland and Zoë Bennett, "Action Is the Life of All: The Bible and Practical Theology," *Contact* no. 150 (January 1, 2006): 8–17.

discusses common ways in which Christian traditioning processes incorporate new information into theology and praxis. Chapter 2 turns directly to the archaeological research of the Hebrew Highland Settlements, providing an in-depth discussion of the artifacts and how they are interpreted. The chapter provides a consolidation of the various research across archaeology, Ancient Near Eastern studies, and biblical studies. The various ways that Highland Settlements material contradicts or aligns with certain biblical texts are considered.

Chapter 3 examines the historical and political context of the conquest story in the book of Joshua by answering these questions: If the Israelite conquest did not take place, then why was this story told? Who wrote the conquest story and why? Many biblical scholars take up these questions and provide historical and social political interpretations of these texts. This research helps to demystify the violence in the conquest narrative and enable readers of the Bible to make interpretive decisions about how they read the story. Chapter 3 also discusses ways that the conquest story is interwoven in the fabric of the US social imagination, surveying how the story has shaped imagination in a variety of violent realities across Western colonial cultures both past and present.

Chapter 4 provides a feminist theological analysis of the Highland Settlements and interprets them as a liberating counterhistory that supports a counternarrative to an Israelite conquest of Canaan. The chapter explores ways that the Highland Settlements material can be read alongside the exodus story and provides fresh insights into this foundational biblical narrative. The chapter invites insights from feminist theology and understandings of history, cultural memory studies, and graphic design to interpret the significance of the Highland Settlements for reshaping religious imagination and church transformation.

Conclusion

Many people and institutions are beginning to confront their racist and colonial histories. Old wounds are rising to the surface with a force no longer ignorable. The church must confront its complicity in these wounds if it is ever to live into its own best ideals. The same is true for the United States. The Highland Settlements represent one salve for a long and entangled historical wound. The settlements story challenges the biblical conquest narrative that undergirds imperialistic, racist, and genocidal Christian imaginaries. The retelling of Hebrew origins made possible through the Highland Settlements discoveries prompts a reckoning of the past and invokes new Christian imagination in the present. It is not often that new information reveals the origins of the biblical faith traditions differently. It is time to integrate the Highland Settlements story into the Christian story.

1

History
and
Social Change

⌒

The conquest narrative was overtly present in the ideology and events of the January 6, 2021, insurrection in Washington, DC, when a group called the Jericho March organized people to protest the 2020 presidential election. During the Jericho March, "Christians gathered in D.C., blowing shofars, the ram's horn typically used in Jewish worship, to banish the 'darkness of election fraud' and ensure that 'the walls of corruption crumble.'[1] The conquest narrative is alive and well in United States.

The United States is considered secular, but it is a veneered secularity. Christian theological themes interweave US history and its ethos so deeply that they are hardly noticeable. Latent theological themes, myths, and doctrines—like the Protestant work ethic, Manifest Destiny, the myth of progress, and the Doctrine of Discovery—come from a Christian theological imagination that generates the scaffolds of the dominant US

---

[1]Emma Green, "A Christian Insurrection," *The Atlantic*, January 8, 2021.

ethos.[2] Scratch the surface of these underlying theological themes, and, not far below, the conquest narrative rests.

The Israelite conquest of Canaan provided religious and psychological scaffolding for the European colonization and conquest of North America.[3] Puritan preachers referred to Native Americans as Canaanites, or peoples "worthy of annihilation."[4] Puritans, however, identified themselves as the "chosen people," a new Israel, and viewed America as part of their divine destiny.[5] This same ideology drove the US

---

[2]See the following: L. Daniel Hawk, *Joshua in 3-D: A Commentary on Biblical Conquest and Manifest Destiny* (Eugene, OR: Cascade, 2010); Richard T. Wright, *Myths America Lives By* (Champaign: University of Illinois, 2004); Reginald Horsman, *Race and Manifest Destiny: Origins of American Racial Anglo-Saxonism* (Cambridge, MA: Harvard University Press, 1981). The following discusses Christian themes and the Doctrine of Discovery: Stephen T. Newcomb, *Pagans in the Promised Land* (Golden, CO: Fulcrum, 2008).

[3]For example, see William G. Dever, *Who Were the Early Israelites and Where Did They Come From?* (Grand Rapids: Eerdmans, 2003), ix; Grace Jantzen, *Violence to Eternity*, ed. Jeremy Carrette and Morny Joy (London: Routledge, 2009), 6; Willie James Jennings, *The Christian Imagination: Theology and the Origins of Race* (New Haven, CT: Yale University Press, 2010), 207–94; Robert Warrior, "Canaanites, Cowboys, and Indians," *Christianity & Crisis* 49, no. 12 (September 11, 1989): 7.

[4]As Robert Warrior explains, "Many Puritan preachers were fond of referring to Native Americans as Amelekites and Canaanites—in other words, people who, if they would not be converted, were worthy of annihilation. By examining such instances in theological and political writings, in sermons, and elsewhere, we can understand how America's self-image as a 'chosen people' has provided a rhetoric to mystify domination." Warrior, "Canaanites, Cowboys, and Indians," 3.

[5]Sacvan Bercovitch shows how a Puritan ideology enabled the colonists to view the extermination of Native Americans with impunity. He argues that the "Puritans, despite their missionary pretenses, regarded the country as theirs and its natives as an obstacle to their destiny as Americans. They could remove that obstacle either by conversion (followed by 'confinement'), or else by extermination. Since the former course proved insecure, they had recourse to the latter." Sacvan Bercovitch, *The Puritan Origins of the American Self* (New Haven, CT: Yale University Press, 2011), 141.

myth of Manifest Destiny, which infers that Europeans had the divine right to a westward expansion of North America, taking land and killing Indigenous Peoples with impunity, just as God empowered the Israelites to do in the book of Joshua.[6] Whatever the intention or function of the conquest narrative in its original context, it is embroiled in the violence that has shaped the United States.[7]

Social justice movements in the United States must deal with the underlying violent mythology of conquest, or this story will continue to empower supremacy, violence, and division as was evident at the Jericho March on January 6. Because Christianity is interwoven into the fabric of America, changing Christian imagination can help reshape broader culture. The Highland Settlements archaeological evidence opens a historical vista that challenges the story of conquest and can generate a new historical Christian imagination with a foundation of liberation rather than violence. Christianity is neither monolithic nor unchanging. New insights on the past provide resources for shaping Christian imagination, theology, and practice today.[8] The church has a long history

---

[6]L. Daniel Hawk traces how the book of Joshua has informed prominent ideology in the United States. Hawk, *Joshua in 3-D.*

[7]Grace Jantzen discusses the danger of the biblical stories of conquest when they "are read, as they have been repeatedly in Western history, as a factual account, indeed as divine revelation, then it is open to anyone who puts themselves into the position of the chosen ones to do violence to those whom they deem to be excluded. . . . It is an ideology that has had a long afterlife in the history of the West." See Jantzen, *Violence to Eternity*, 98.

[8]For example, the ecclesiological projects of Kelly Brown Douglas, Elisabeth Schüssler Fiorenza, Delores Williams, Grace Jantzen, and Rosemary Radford Ruether, to name a few, delve into historical resources as a key focus in their projects. Douglas, *Sexuality and the Black Church: A Womanist Perspective* (Maryknoll, NY: Orbis Books, 1999); Douglas, *Black Bodies and the Black Church: A Blues Slant* (New York: Palgrave Macmillan, 2012); Jantzen, *Violence to Eternity*; Ruether, *Sexism and God-Talk: Toward a Femi-*

of evolving by incorporating new information and theological insights as they arise. Change has been part of the process since the beginning.

History and Politics

History is power. History can change the status quo. Political battles are currently being waged over which version of US history can be taught in public schools. Teaching US history in ways that account for white supremacy, genocide, slavery, and other atrocities empowers marginalized groups to contest unjust institutions and ways of being. Ethnic studies courses in public schools incorporate multicultural curriculums that affirm minority students' cultural identities and histories, while also "supporting their critical consciousness development and engagement in praxis."[9] The *New York Times*' publication of The 1619 Project "aims to reframe the country's history by placing the consequences of slavery and the contributions of black Americans at the very center of our national narrative."[10] The 1619 Project shifts the historical

---

nist Theology (Boston: Beacon Press, 1993); Schüssler Fiorenza, *In Memory of Her: A Feminist Theological Reconstruction of Christian Origins* (New York: Crossroad, 1994); Williams, *Sisters in the Wilderness: The Challenge of Womanist God-Talk* (Maryknoll, NY: Orbis Books, 2013).

[9]Keisha L. Green, Kysa Nygreen, Laura A. Valdiviezo, and Joel Ariel Arce, "Teacher Professional Development for Ethnic Studies: A Critical Youth-Centered Approach," *Multicultural Perspectives* 22, no. 3 (July 2020): 139. The authors explain that "ethnic studies teaching positively impacts students' academic motivation and achievement" (139).

[10]"The *1619 Project* is an ongoing initiative from The New York Times Magazine that began in August 2019, the 400th anniversary of the beginning of American slavery. It aims to reframe the country's history by placing the consequences of slavery and the contributions of black Americans at the very

US narrative away from a sugarcoated version that highlights European colonists' achievements rather than facing the brutal history of enslavement and genocide that make up the bloody, violent cornerstones of US history. Such change is rejected by those maintaining hegemonic power to the point of violence. The events of January 6, 2021, and other white-supremacist actions in our current time, cannot be separated from the coalescence of marginalized groups gaining power, claiming their own histories and the right to exist.

The *1619 Project* was countered by a disturbingly racist document published on the last day of the Trump presidency called *The 1776 Report*.[11] This is a largely inaccurate rendition of the founding of the United States that dodges any accountability for long-lasting harms of enslavement, Jim Crow, and the plight of women and queer people.[12] The current white supremacist backlash, or the battle against "woke," as Florida governor Ron DeSantis describes it, has led to legislation banning critical race theories and books that address race, sexuality, and the rise in violent rhetoric and crimes. These are all battles in a larger war for control of the status quo.[13] This backlash indicates that origin stories matter. If the United

---

center of our national narrative." The 1619 Project, "The 1619 Project," *New York Times*, August 14, 2019.

[11]Michael Crowley and Jennifer Schuessler, "Trump's 1776 Commission Critiques Liberalism in Report Derided by Historians," *New York Times*, January 19, 2021; AHA Council, "AHA Condemns Report of Advisory 1776 Commission," American Historical Society, January 20, 2021; Gillian Brockell, " 'A Hack Job,' 'Outright Lies': Trump Commission's '1776 Report' Outrages Historians," *Washington Post*, January 19, 2021.

[12]Brockell, " 'A Hack Job.' "

[13]Janice Gassam Asare, "The War on Critical Race Theory Continues as Some Call It Anti-White," *Forbes*, May 9, 2021; Laura Meckler and Hannah Natanson, "As Schools Expand Racial Equity Work, Conservatives See a New Threat in Critical Race Theory," *Washington Post*, May 3, 2021.

States is truly "in a battle for the soul of this nation," as President Joe Biden declared, then the frontlines of this battle face the past.[14] History matters.

In this political context, a newly discovered history of Israel, one that challenges conquest and highlights the liberation struggles of a people living on the outskirts of empire, is important. The Highland Settlements are an example of a history that can prompt radical imagination with the potential to reshape Christian social imaginaries, interrupting the deep-rooted story of conquest in the US social imagination. The Highland Settlements provide new answers to identity questions pertaining to the biblical faith traditions such as: Who are we? How did we get here? Answering these questions differently can catalyze radical imagination and social change.

Social Imagination

Social imagination or "the social imaginary" is a useful concept for exploring social change processes, including the influences that new histories and new insights on the past have on the present. Social imagination is a way of describing a collective symbol or meaning system that is shared across a large group of people.[15] Symbol systems function through

---

[14]Biden has repeatedly used the phrase "battle for the soul of the nation," during his 2020 campaign and in his presidential speeches, to signify the importance of keeping American democracy strong and rejecting an American autocracy.

[15]Cornelius Castoriadis, political scientist and psychoanalyst, is considered the first theorist to bring forth the concept of social imagination. See Cornelius Castoriadis, *The Imaginary Institution of Society* (Cambridge, MA: MIT Press, 1998). Subsequent works in social imagination, such as from Charles Taylor and Benedict Anderson, draw upon Castoriadis. For example, Anderson argues that the creation of the modern nation-state was only possible after the rise of

imagination. Symbols are things that represent something else. A symbol requires imagination, the capacity to see a thing other than it is, to connect two disparate things.[16] Written language exemplifies symbolic imagination. In English, the letters c, a, and t, placed in this order, create the word "cat," which, when read, evokes an image of the furry, sometimes friendly, four-legged animal. It takes imagination to connect the word "cat" to the fluffy animal. Institutions also depend on symbol systems to function. For example, the economy, justice system, and religions are socially sanctioned symbol systems: they connect symbols to practices that create a status quo.[17]

Groups of people create a shared social imagination or social imaginary when they interpret the same symbols in similar ways. Social imaginaries can consist of symbols, myths, and stories that convey commonly shared meaning and can create social norms, identity, shared practices, and group cohesiveness.[18] Social imaginaries mediate social norms and shape human interactions, enabling people to "imagine their social existence, how they fit together with others."[19] For ex-

---

print media—specifically the newspaper and the novel—because engagement with newly emerging narrative forms generated a new type of social imaginary. See Benedict R. O'G. Anderson, *Imagined Communities: Reflections on the Origin and Spread of Nationalism*, rev. ed. (London: Verso, 2016).

[16]Castoriadis, *The Imaginary Institution of Society*, 127.

[17]Castoriadis, *The Imaginary Institution of Society*, 117.

[18]Social imagination "makes possible common practice and a widely shared sense of legitimacy." Charles Taylor, *Modern Social Imaginaries* (Durham, NC: Duke University Press, 2004), 23. See also Castoriadis, *The Imaginary Institution of Society*, 117.

[19]Taylor, *Modern Social Imaginaries*, 23. Taylor argues that social imagination enables people to "imagine their social existence, how they fit together with others." Cooke and Macy also argue that imagination "has the power to carry meaning, arouse emotion, and influence action." Bernard J. Cooke and Gary Macy, *Christian Symbol and Ritual: An Introduction* (New York: Oxford University Press, 2005), 10.

ample, a nation-state's flag can convey complex meanings of national identity, a particular geography, nationalism, patriotism, loyalty, or fear to name only a few possible associations. Even within the same social imaginaries, people can interpret symbols in diverse and even disparate ways.

Radical Imagination

Social imaginaries are not static.[20] Change happens as new images arise, creating a radical social imagination that shatters old ways of being in an ever-ongoing process.[21] Radical social imagination causes people to rethink basic identity questions, leading to a change in their perception and expectations. This process causes individuals and communities to begin to question the status quo, imagining other ways of doing and being. When this happens, societies and institutions "self-alter."[22]

As "self" suggests, radical imagination does not occur in a vacuum. New narrations of the past are integral to both individual and societal transformation. When an individual interprets the past differently, they can compose a new life

---

[20]Cooke and Macy, *Christian Symbol and Ritual,* 10.

[21]Social imaginaries typically operate tacitly and are not usually reflected upon until social change occurs. For new images to impact the status quo, they must not come "out of nowhere"; new images must emerge from within the existing symbol system in order to make sense. If new images do not connect with the status quo, then they risk being illegible or too extreme by delegitimizing too much of the current symbol system. However, new images that emerge from within the existing symbol system but suggest something different can shape a new status quo. Castoriadis names the in-breaking of a new image that can shape imagination the "radical imaginary." Castoriadis, *The Imaginary Institution of Society,* 372.

[22]Castoriadis, *The Imaginary Institution of Society,* 146–47.

story and imagine a different future.[23] This same premise applies to social groups. New images that inspire social change cannot come 'out of nowhere,' for they must be legible within existing social imaginaries and only make a small improvisation.[24] Too extreme of an image will delegitimize the current imaginary and not be incorporated by the collective. Historical discoveries are typically legible within existing social imaginaries because they provide a new image of the past while maintaining the basic structures of the existing symbol system.[25]

Christianity and the Hebrew Tradition

Christianity itself emerged through radical imagination and a social change process, growing out of a "popular" Jewish movement from the Galilee region.[26] It did not develop in a cultural or religious vacuum but was very much embedded in Hebrew tradition. The religious imaginaries of Judaism informed Jesus's conception of the Divine, his daily practices, and his critiques of the Roman Empire and the Jerusalem Temple system. The Israelite tradition and the Torah are foundational for Christian tradition because the Christian *ekklesia* grew from Judaism. As part of a popular movement

---

[23]Rebecca Chopp talks about this type of change as a social therapeutic process. See Rebecca S. Chopp, "Christian Moral Imagination: A Feminist Practical Theology and the Future of Theological Education," *International Journal of Practical Theology* 1, no. 1 (January 1, 1997): 106.

[24]Castoriadis, *The Imaginary Institution of Society,* 372.

[25]Chopp, "Christian Moral Imagination," 106.

[26]Richard A. Horsley, *Jesus and Empire: The Kingdom of God and the New World Disorder* (Minneapolis: Fortress, 2003). See chapter 2, "Resistance and Rebellion in Judea and Galilee," for a detailed discussion of the "popular" Jewish movement from the Galilee region.

within Judaism, early churches presupposed Hebrew traditions and biblical texts and often incorporated them, implicitly and explicitly, into early Christian traditions. Catherine Keller convincingly argues that it "is the Hebrew tradition of the love of the stranger that seems to have served as Jesus's hermeneutical test and key, opening up the stranger love of the indecent and of the enemy."[27] At the same time, Jesus and his followers offered a reappraisal of that Hebrew heritage on certain points, prompted by the demands of new circumstances and new evidence. Importantly, they did not step out of the tradition to do this. Their reconfigurations occurred within the existing symbol systems of the Hebrew religious tradition.

Peter's dream described in Acts 10:9:29 is a prime New Testament example of this dynamic. This episode demonstrates how the emerging Christian tradition was wrestling with the Hebrew tradition it inherited, specifically regarding the relationship between Jewish and Gentile peoples. Peter's dream sparked a new vision that reshaped the existing tradition for a new context. The dream revealed to Peter that even though Hebrew tradition and Scriptures prescribed certain dietary laws, God—the same God witnessed to in Hebrew tradition and Scriptures—was now declaring that previously forbidden foods were clean (Acts 10:11–16). Upon awakening, Peter applied this message not only to food, but also to Jewish and Gentile human relationships.

After his dream and subsequent shift in perspective, Peter visited the Roman centurion Cornelius, who had summoned him. Peter explained his decision to see Cornelius, a Gentile: "You yourselves know that it is unlawful for a Jew to asso-

---

[27]Catherine Keller, *Intercarnations: Exercises in Theological Possibility* (New York: Fordham University Press, 2017), 28.

ciate with or to visit a Gentile; but God has shown me that I should not call anyone profane or unclean. So when I was sent for, I came without objection" (Acts 10:28–29). Peter's dream, laden with theological symbolism that he could understand from within the context of his received tradition and the practical theological changes he made in his Jewish practice, are examples of the traditioning process at work in early Christian movements. The historical Hebrew basis of these movements equipped them with the means to critique and modify its perception of historical—and present—reality.

In addition to drawing on the Hebrew traditions and Scriptures, elements from within the historical Christian traditions are themselves drawn upon and reimagined in Christian traditioning processes. For example, the four marks of the church in the Nicene Creed—one, holy, catholic, and apostolic—have been the subject of frequent theological reflection in times of theological conflict and church divisions. Theologians have, at times, put forward specific interpretations of the four marks of the church in order to quell conflict and assert an orthodoxy over and against competing views.[28] Each new interpretation of the historical four marks can bring a new vision or practice to contemporary contexts. What is important for our purposes here is that the church's interpretive process precisely involves a retelling of the stories we have received in a way that remains true to the symbols of our tradition, while also drawing on changes in perspective

---

[28]For example, Gordon Lathrop and Timothy Wengert show that the four marks of the church became prominent during the Protestant Reformation within various ecclesiological debates. As they explain, "The marks of the church arose in a very specific polemical situation where Luther's opponents forced him to reevaluate his ecclesiology along evangelical lines." Gordon Lathrop and Timothy J. Wengert, *Christian Assembly: Marks of the Church in a Pluralistic Age* (Minneapolis: Fortress, 2004), 19.

and circumstance to adjust how we deploy the language of our religious past to meet present needs.

Contemporary theological projects continue to incorporate new insights rooted in the past to refine engagement with the past in response to present realities. For example, feminist theology has a rich tradition of examining history as a source for reshaping Christian imagination to prompt liberative theology and practice. Prominent theologians such as Elisabeth Schüssler Fiorenza and Letty Russell often turned to the early Jesus movements and practices of the newly emerging ekklesia to incorporate historical insights from these sources into new visions for what it means to be the church.[29] What is

---

[29]Feminist reconstructions of the early Jesus movements were an important stream in feminist biblical scholarship and theology particularly in the 1970s through 1990s, having a broad reach across academic and ecclesial audiences alike. See, for example: Letty Russell, *Church in the Round: Feminist Interpretation of the Church* (Louisville, KY: Westminster/John Knox, 1993); Elisabeth Schüssler Fiorenza, *Discipleship of Equals: A Critical Feminist Ekklesia-ology of Liberation* (New York: Crossroad, 1994); Elisabeth Schüssler Fiorenza, *In Memory of Her: A Feminist Theological Reconstruction of Christian Origins*, 10th ann. ed. (New York: Crossroad, 1994). There have also been later critiques by some scholars who contend that the early Jesus movements were not any more liberative for women than other Greco-Roman groups or institutions. For example, see Kathleen E. Corley, *Women and the Historical Jesus: Feminist Myths of Christian Origins* (Santa Rosa, CA: Polebridge, 2002); John H. Elliott, "Jesus Was Not an Egalitarian: A Critique of an Anachronistic and Idealist Theory," *Biblical Theology Bulletin* 32 (2002): 75–91; John H. Elliott, "The Jesus Movement Was Not Egalitarian but Family-Oriented," *Biblical Interpretation* 11 (2003): 173–210. Others argue that the early Jesus movements articulated an egalitarian or even utopian ideal that, whether fully implemented in practice or not, still has revolutionary power in terms of shaping imagination in the present. See, for example, Elizabeth A. Castelli, "The Ekklesia of Women and/as Utopian Space: Locating the Work of Elisabeth Schüssler Fiorenza in Feminist Utopian Thought," in Jane Schaberg, Alice Bach, and Ester Fuchs, eds., *On the Cutting Edge: The Study of Women in Biblical Worlds: Essays in Honor of Elisabeth Schüssler Fiorenza* (New York: Continuum, 2004), 36–52.

more, the rootedness of the Jesus movement in the historical reality of Judaism reemerges here. Schüssler Fiorenza interprets the connection between Judaism and early Christianity, stating that the "praxis and vision of Jesus and his movement is best understood as an inner-Jewish renewal movement."[30] She argues that Jesus's ministry emerged from a "critical feminist impulse" found within Judaism.[31] Because Jesus was inspirited by his Jewish tradition, an important source for a feminist historical perspective is the broader Hebrew tradition and the liberative "critical feminist impulses" found there.[32] Such historical explorations complement the already robust theological work that retrieves liberative elements in the Jesus movements and early ekklesia.[33]

Feminists are not alone in seeing the connection between studies of ancient Judaism and Christian theology. For example, Bryan Stone observes that the term "ekklesia" meant "democratic assembly," but, in the Christian context, it also pointed toward the Hebrew tradition of the Israelite assembly

---

[30]Schüssler Fiorenza, *In Memory of Her*, 107. It should be noted that Jewish feminist Judith Plaskow critiqued early ideas of Christian egalitarianism as anti-Jewish in their understandings of early Christianity as over and against early Judaism. See Judith Plaskow, "Anti-Judaism in Christian Feminist Interpretation," in Elisabeth Schüssler Fiorenza, ed., *Searching the Scriptures: A Feminist Introduction* (New York: Crossroad, 1993), 117–29. In response, feminist Christian theologians such as Schüssler Fiorenza emphasize that the early Jesus movements rather than being against Judaism actually drew on a critical feminist impulse found within Judaism itself. See, for example, Elisabeth Schüssler Fiorenza, "Jesus, Women, and Christian Anti-Judaism," in *Jesus and the Politics of Interpretation* (New York: Continuum, 2000), 39, 67–96.

[31]Schüssler Fiorenza, *In Memory of Her*, 107.

[32]Schüssler Fiorenza, *In Memory of Her*, 107.

[33]Some churches already draw on feminine images of God from the Hebrew tradition, such as Sophia or Lady Wisdom, into liturgical settings. While these images of God were not prominent in patriarchal Christian settings, many churches are resuscitating them and incorporating them into their theologies and practices.

as the people of God.[34] As such, the term "ekklesia" intrinsically linked community building in early Christian ecclesiology with community building in Judaism: "Any fully adequate understanding of Christian ecclesiology would need, therefore, to explore Hebrew modes of community that predate Christianity and account for the church's early and ongoing relation to Judaism."[35] The Highland Settlements evidence reveals the earliest known mode of Hebrew community building, which would eventually lead to the development of Israelite identity, Scriptures, and traditions. From this standpoint, the Highland Settlements can be a valuable source for understanding more ancient forms of Hebrew community building, which can contribute to understanding historical ecclesiology to refine understandings of the church in the present.

Despite their influence on Christian tradition and imagination, no significant study has looked to the origins of the Hebrew tradition as revealed in the Highland Settlements materials as a resource for Christian imagination and theology. Some may argue that such a project has no relevance for Christianity since the Highland Settlements predate the biblical traditions. However, archaeological findings like these settlements carry immense implications for our understanding of those biblical traditions and can refine our understanding of the textual tradition, impacting our engagement with the Bible and how we let it shape us. Hebrew origins, it turns out, are immensely important for Christian self-conception

---

[34]Stone explains that "the historical genesis of the church is not to be found primarily in Greco-Roman culture or its various social institutions, but in Judaism itself. Just as important . . . is the way the term ecclesia linked early Christians with Israel as a nation and as the people of God." Bryan P. Stone, *A Reader in Ecclesiology*, Ashgate Contemporary Ecclesiology (Burlington, VT: Ashgate, 2012), 3.

[35]Stone, *A Reader in Ecclesiology*, 3.

because Christianity receives the origin stories of Judaism regarding Israel's history and inhabitance in the promised land as its own. Because of the inherent connection between Judaism and Christianity, the origins of the Hebrew people are also of importance for Christian traditioning processes. The precedent of the Christian traditioning process itself is one reason to bring forward the Highland Settlements history. Drawing on the Highland Settlements evidence follows a historical traditioning pattern that has been part of Christian life and churches since the beginning.

Some might argue that drawing on biblical texts and other prominent elements from within Christian history, like the Nicene Creed, is not the same as drawing on the Highland Settlements, because ecclesial communities have been drawing on biblical texts and creeds for centuries, whereas the Highland Settlements archaeological evidence has not been incorporated into ecclesial traditioning processes in any prominent way thus far. This argument is not a good reason to exclude it. Just as new insights in historical awareness (such as evidenced in feminist scholarship on what early Christians understood by ekklesia as a response against centuries of patriarchal conceptualizations of church) and new perspectives from historical contexts (such as the early church's incorporation of Gentiles, prompting a reinterpretation of scriptural laws) have continually refined Christians' appropriation of their religious past, new discoveries can offer fresh inspiration and should not be ignored simply because they are recently unearthed.

Incorporating New Discoveries

Incorporating new discoveries into existing traditions can be a time-consuming and challenging process. This process,

however, can invite fresh perspectives of theological reflection, providing enriching textures and insights on the past and
present. The Highland Settlements archaeological evidence is
not the only new discovery in the last century that is currently
being incorporated into the Christian imagination and broader
cultural imagination. One example is particularly instructive.
The ancient Nag Hammadi texts have influenced the American religious landscape since their discovery in 1945.[36] They
contain parts of fifty-two fourth- and fifth-century texts and
provide new ways of interpreting Christian symbols, in part
because they provide a countermemory of ancient Christianity
that is not contained in dominant orthodox traditions. Sometimes, the Nag Hammadi texts even subvert these traditions.[37]
The Nag Hammadi texts help reimagine Christian origins in
meaningful ways by opening a new dialogue into the ancient
Christian past, which, by virtue of the church's still-prominent
role in society, impacts people in the present.[38]

The Nag Hammadi texts provide a window into the multiple forms of Christianity that existed in the first and second
centuries but were repressed in the second and third centuries by a powerful hierarchical orthodoxy that railed against
differing beliefs.[39] The Nag Hammadi texts offer alternative

---

[36]Dillon explains that the English translations of the Nag Hammadi texts
were fully published in 1977 and have steadily been making their way into the
American religious landscape. Matthew J. Dillon, "The Heretical Revival: The
Nag Hammadi Library in American Religion and Culture" (PhD dissertation,
Rice University, 2017), 7.

[37]Dillon, "The Heretical Revival," 212. Dillon draws on Jan Assmann's idea
of a "return of the repressed" cultural memory in highlighting how the Nag
Hammadi texts have been received in certain religious contexts in America.

[38]Elaine Pagels explains that "[b]y investigating the texts from Nag Hammadi, we can see how politics and religion coincide in the development of
Christianity." Elaine Pagels, *The Gnostic Gospels* (New York: Random House,
1979), xxxvi; Dillon, "The Heretical Revival," 7, 213.

[39]Pagels, *The Gnostic Gospels*, 149.

theological and historical perspectives on the early church that can challenge dominant Christian traditions. Today, people who find themselves questioning dominant orthodox theologies and perspectives on what constitutes and legitimates authority, particularly as related to sacred texts, are drawn to the Nag Hammadi texts.[40] The far-reaching impact of the Nag Hammadi texts in an American Christian context includes "new conceptions of the Christian canon, new ritual practices, revised theological positions from Christian readers and writers, and new positions on sexuality, gender, and personhood within the American-Christian context."[41] Study of the Nag Hammadi texts invites theological discussions on concepts that were debated in early Christianity about Christ, the resurrection, and women's participation in leadership, to name only a few.[42]

The Nag Hammadi texts are generating fresh perspectives within and outside of the church. Hal Taussig has taught over two hundred Nag Hammadi text studies across many different churches and discovered that people are excited, refreshed, and intrigued by the texts.[43] Taussig also reports that people experienced a deepening in their faith by studying them and that many people wanted to integrate the Nag Hammadi texts with traditional ideas as they searched for "alternative spiritual paths while still holding onto traditions of the past."[44] Taussig's teaching of the Nag Hammadi texts led him to

---

[40]Pagels, *The Gnostic Gospels*, 150.

[41]Dillon, "The Heretical Revival," 213.

[42]Pagels, *The Gnostic Gospels*, 150.

[43]Ray Olson, "A New New Testament: A Reinvented Bible for the 21st Century Combining Traditional and Newly Discovered Texts," *The Booklist* 109, no. 13 (March 1, 2013): 4.

[44]Hal Taussig, *A New New Testament: A Bible for the Twenty-First Century Combining Traditional and Newly Discovered Texts* (Boston: Mariner / Houghton Mifflin Harcourt, 2015), xi.

develop *A New New Testament: A Reinvented Bible for the 21st Century Combining Traditional and Newly Discovered Texts,* incorporating ten Nag Hammadi texts into the New Testament canon and inviting readers on an "inspiring, and well-informed journey through the very early writings of those in the legacy of Jesus."[45] The Nag Hammadi texts illuminate the New Testament texts by giving readers an awareness that other texts exist that were not included in dominant biblical canons.[46]

The Nag Hammadi texts give people access to what is *outside* the canon, so that they, in turn, can understand the biblical canon better. They cast into relief the entire process of "canonization" in the early church, showing how fluid of a process it was. They further reinforce the reality of early Christianity's diversity of thought and practice—an insight which, in turn, can lead us to see with fresh eyes the staggering amount of diversity within the canon itself.

Like the Nag Hammadi texts, the Highland Settlements archaeological evidence provides an alternative counterhistory or countermemory of ancient Hebrew history that is not explicit within the biblical canon. The Highland Settlements archaeological evidence invites theological reflection because it provides insight into patterns of Canaanite settlement that are outside the Hebrew Bible canon. In some instances, the Highland Settlements material already prompts new perspectives and deeper theological reflection. Like the Nag Hammadi

---

[45]Taussig, *A New New Testament*, xviii.

[46]John Dominic Crossan explains in the preface to Taussig's book that "what you do with that knowledge, and how you judge between texts in or out, is a separate issue. But you should know that *all* gospel versions were not taken, that a selection was made, that some were accepted, and others rejected. And that knowledge is, to repeat, an education, and education is about knowing options." Taussig, *A New New Testament*, xi.

texts, when the Highland Settlements evidence has been introduced in educational settings, it has prompted excitement, inspiration to political and social activists, and a desire for additional knowledge. Just as Hal Taussig noticed the excitement generated when he taught on the Nag Hammadi texts, several biblical scholars observed similar phenomena when teaching people about the Highland Settlements evidence.

Tribes *Moments*

David Jobling has named the profound reactions he witnessed when people encountered the Highland Settlement materials for the first time, calling it a *"Tribes* moment," referring to Norman Gottwald's book, *The Tribes of Yahweh*.[47] Jobling notes that, when people learned about the egalitarian or heterarchical ethos of the ancient proto-Israelites, they linked it to their own ideas of liberation.[48] Gottwald himself discussed how the Highland Settlements inspired political and religious activists around the globe, noting responses from readers who were political prisoners and passed *Tribes* around from cell to cell and considered it a holy book, and Latin American Roman Catholic nuns who created flip charts of Highland Settlements material to inspire their base communities.[49] These are only a few examples of how audiences around the world have been inspired by the Highland Settlements evidence presented in Gottwald's groundbreaking tome.

Gottwald's and Jobling's stories suggest that Highland

---

[47]David Jobling, "Specters of *Tribes*: On the 'Revenance' of a Classic," in *Tracking* The Tribes of Yahweh: *On the Trail of a Classic* (London: Sheffield Academic, 2002), 15.

[48]Jobling, "Specters of *Tribes*," 15.

[49]Gottwald, "Response to Contributors," 181; Gottwald, " 'Political Activism and Biblical Scholarship: An Interview,'" 166–67.

Settlements research captures the imagination of people across a broad swath of social and religious locations. This is a promising phenomenon, like what Hal Taussig experienced when he taught the Nag Hammadi texts to a variety of audiences. The Highland Settlements should be incorporated into the ongoing Christian traditioning processes because they invite richer theological reflection and questions around Hebrew origins.[50]

Confronting Legacies of Violence

Christian traditioning processes have always operated in tandem with both the received historical tradition and ongoing developments in historical awareness. Currently, conversations about history are happening within the church and the broader US context. Many institutions are beginning to deal openly with a long legacy of racist and imperialistic domination, oppression, and injustice. The Black Lives Matter movement calls to account years of police brutality and the unjust killings of Black people at the hands of the police and the systemic oppression of Black, Indigenous, and other peoples of color (BIPOC) around the country. Across the United States, monuments to Confederate leaders and slave owners are being pulled down, and racist corporate logos and sports teams' names are changing. This is a time for individuals and institutions to reckon with their imperialistic and racist pasts and present. It calls to consciousness the recurring crises of racism, sexism, and imperialism in the United States and subsequent social justice movements. The United States has a long and torrid history of injustice.

---

[50]This does not necessarily mean inviting all new discoveries into preexisting "canons." It can, however, mean inviting new discoveries into Christian traditioning processes in order to learn what new light they can shed on the existing religious tradition even if they do not become part of a broader canon.

Seeking Change

Regardless of whether a church identifies theologically as progressive or conservative, many Western churches in the United States can trace their lineage within US settler-colonialism and, before that, European imperialism. Because of this violent legacy, churches must seek repentance, reparations, and reconciliation where possible as a form of social therapy. Churches are beginning such therapeutic work. In July 2022, Pope Francis embarked on a "penitential pilgrimage" to Canada to publicly apologize to Indigenous Peoples for the forced placement of Indigenous children in Catholic boarding schools, where they suffered physical and sexual abuse and were forced to assimilate to European Christian culture. "I humbly beg forgiveness for the evil committed by so many Christians against the Indigenous peoples," Francis said.[51]

In 2021, the Episcopal Diocese of Massachusetts put forward *A Toolkit for Reparations in Community: A Resource for the Body of Christ*, which provides congregations with resources to discuss the Episcopal Church's historic ties to slavery, processes toward reparations, and other resources.[52] In 2022, the same diocese voted to create a reparations fund with the goal of reaching $11.1 million in the fund.[53] At a more local level, the United Parish in Brookline launched the Negro Spirituals Royalties project, in which the church

[51]Nicole Winfield and Peter Smith, "Pope Apologizes for 'Catastrophic' School Policy in Canada," AP News, July 26, 2022.

[52]The Reparations Toolkit was prompted by the larger Episcopal Church declaration in 2020 that charged churches to deal with reparations in their own community. "Reparations Toolkit | Episcopal Diocese of Massachusetts," Episcopal Diocese of Massachusetts, 2023.

[53]Tracy J. Sukraw, "Massachusetts Diocese Creates Reparations Fund with $11.1 Million Goal," *Episcopal News Service* (blog), November 16, 2022.

pays royalties for the use of Negro spirituals in worship services.[54] The church partners with a Boston-based nonprofit,
Hamilton-Garrett Music and Arts, "dedicated to passing on
and preserving the legacy of Black music," that receives the
royalty funds.[55] These are just three examples among many.
They represent positive steps toward broader systemic change
that is needed to counter centuries of harm.

Confronting violent pasts, telling liberative histories, and
seeking repair for past harms is a form of social therapy that
will necessarily result in tearing down harmful monuments
of the past and reimaging history and contemporary praxis in
ways that reconcile injustices and seek the flourishing of all
people.[56] While these are complicated processes, challenging
the history of conquest embedded within Christianity and centering the newly discovered liberative history of the Highland
Settlements can be an important early step. New histories
can reshape imagination and identity, effecting and affecting
social change. Churches must challenge the historicity of the
conquest narrative and center the liberative history of the
Highland Settlements as we confront legacies of Christian
violence, reshape harmful Christian imaginaries, and create
more just churches.

---

[54]The United Parish is a merged congregation that maintains ties with the
United Church of Christ, the United Methodist Church, and the American
Baptist Church.

[55]Abby Patkin, "Listen: Brookline Church Embraces Power of Negro
Spirituals," Wicked Local, November 2, 2021.

[56]Rebecca Chopp argues that practical theology can aid in the work of
transformation by acting as a form of social therapy, which "investigates
and excavates the past, seeing points of connection, correlation, relation and
works to make a new, and more adequate, future." Chopp, "Christian Moral
Imagination," 106.

2

Archaeology,
the Bible,
and the
Highland Settlements

❧

Invented and Real Histories

Until the early nineteenth century, the Bible was the primary source for ancient Israelite history. However, archaeological findings, like the discovery of Iron Age I pottery and building foundations, provide an alternative understanding of early Israel's history that reveals places of congruence and contradiction between biblical texts and the archaeological record. Even though the Highland Settlements predate the biblical texts, they are not wholly separate from the Israelite traditions. The Highland Settlements are "proto-Israelite" because they eventually led to a new cultural identity known as Israel.[1] There are remnants and traces of the Highland Settlement

---

[1] William G. Dever, *Who Were the Early Israelites and Where Did They Come From?* (Grand Rapids: Eerdmans, 2003), 194–200; Mario Liverani, *Israel's History and the History of Israel* (London: Routledge, 2014), 58–59.

era within the Hebrew Bible, and archaeological discoveries help to illuminate these scriptural threads. Biblical stories that discuss pre-state Israelite culture provide a window into the Highland Settlements era, when social power was distributed in a heterarchical or even egalitarian way in localized contexts.[2] The archaeological assemblages of material from the Iron Age have congruence with the details of everyday life in Judges and Samuel.[3] The core of Judges contains references to the Highland Settlement period and offers a glimpse into Iron Age I community building, where there was no centralized leadership.[4]

In addition to the stories in Judges, the exodus story (Ex 1–15:21) echoes key themes from the settlement era, and the book of Exodus was likely influenced by the cultural memory of that period.[5] Even though the Iron Age I Highland Settlements predate the writing of the biblical texts, they

---

[2]Norman K. Gottwald, *Politics of Ancient Israel* (Louisville, KY: Westminster John Knox, 2007), 170.

[3]Paula M. McNutt, *Reconstructing the Society of Ancient Israel*, Library of Ancient Israel (Louisville, KY: Westminster John Knox, 1999), 66.

[4]As Dever explains, the "[Judges] narrative consists of stories about everyday life in the formative, *pre-state era*, when 'there was no king in Israel [and] all the people did what was right in their own eyes'" (Judg 21:25). The "pre-state era" that Dever names is the Highland Settlements era. William G. Dever, *Beyond the Texts: An Archaeological Portrait of Ancient Israel and Judah* (Atlanta: SBL Press, 2017), 188. Italics added.

[5]Examples include Linda Stargel, "The Construction of Exodus Identity in the Texts of Ancient Israel: A Social Identity Approach" (Doctor of Philosophy Thesis: The University of Manchester - Nazarene Theological College, 2016); Ronald Hendel, "The Exodus in Biblical Memory," in *Remembering Abraham* (New York: Oxford University Press, 2005), 57–74; Hendrik L. Bosman, "The Exodus as Negotiation of Identity and Human Dignity between Memory and Myth," *HTS Teologiese Studies* 70, no. 1 (January 1, 2014): no. 2709; Nadav Na'aman, "The Exodus Story: Between Historical Memory and Historiographical Composition," *Journal of Ancient Near Eastern Religions* 11, no. 1 (2011): 39–69.

still bore directly on Israelite identity and the ensuing biblical traditions—notably through the exodus story, one of the most important and iconic stories in Hebrew Scripture. The exodus story describes the Israelite people leaving Egypt to escape enslavement and oppression. Similarly, the Highland Settlements evidence points toward Canaanite people leaving Egyptian-ruled Canaanite city-states to escape socioeconomic oppression and even enslavement. Because of these similarities, some argue that many aspects of the biblical exodus story represent the late Bronze Age period of Egyptian imperialism in Canaan and that the biblical exodus story could be a conflation of a broad set of proto-Israelite experiences.[6] Consequently, the Highland Settlements left a tangible imprint on ancient Israelite culture and the biblical texts, which, in turn, shaped Christian traditions.

Furthermore, as archaeological evidence provides a glimpse into Exodus, Judges, and Samuel, it simultaneously contradicts the conquest account of Israelite history found in Joshua. No material evidence supports the biblical depiction of a militaristic invasion of Canaan and the destruction of indigenous Canaanite cities and peoples by the Israelites. Instead, archaeological evidence points to the Highland Settlements and proto-Israelite culture as emerging from within Canaan itself. The archaeological evidence points toward the historiographic or symbolic nature of the history of conquest in the book of Joshua.[7] The discrepancies found between the bibli-

[6]Hendel, *Remembering Abraham*, 62; Na'aman, "The Exodus Story," 68–69; William Henry Propp, *Exodus 19–40: A New Translation with Introduction and Commentary* (New York: Doubleday, 2006), 741.

[7]Liverani, *Israel's History and the History of Israel*, xvi–xvii. Liverani labels the two different Israelite histories (biblical and archaeological) as the "invented or exceptional" or the "real or normal" history. He bases the organization of this book around this premise of Israel's so-called two histories.

cal story of conquest and the Highland Settlements archaeological evidence lead archaeologists and biblical scholars to consider the book of Joshua as a historiographic, "invented or exceptional history" and the archaeological evidence that supports biblical stories found in the book of Judges as a "real or normal history."[8]

Biblical stories recount history in ways that aim to shape culture and contribute to a shared sense of identity. These histories do not report what happened like a news report. As such, interpretation of biblical histories occurs not only by examining the details that the texts provide, but also by attending to the social and political contexts and aims of their authors and editors. Archaeological artifacts, in contrast to written stories, can reveal aspects of what occurred in particular places and times, in ways more reliable than historiographical narratives.[9] For instance, archaeology can establish whether certain places were inhabited during certain time periods. The discovery of habitation patterns and cultural artifacts can reveal something about the identity of the inhabitants. Shards of pottery, tools, stone walls, structural foundations, cultic relics, and burial sites provide details about life in those places and times and offer clues about the people who lived there and then.

For another understanding of these two histories, see also Carol Meyers, *Discovering Eve: Ancient Israelite Women in Context* (Oxford: Oxford University Press, 1991). Meyers refers to these different histories from women's perspectives as (1) the history of the "biblical woman"—that is, the portrayals of women who appear in biblical narratives, which she argues are largely symbolic (e.g., the character Eve); and (2) the history of ordinary "Israelite women" ("Everywoman Eve") revealed by archaeological evidence." To see Meyers's full argument, see chapter 1, "Eve as a Symbol of Women: Understanding the Task," 3–23.

[8]Liverani, *Israel's History and the History of Israel,* xvi–xvii.

[9]Liverani, *Israel's History and the History of Israel,* xvi–xvii, or the history of "everywoman Eve" as Meyers refers to the archaeological evidence as providing: Meyers, *Discovering Eve,* 4–5.

This is not to say that archaeological evidence is neutral, providing only facts. It, too, must be interpreted, or storied, by archaeologists, and this process is never neutral. Just as written history can be shaped to reflect the interests of its authors and editors, archaeological evidence can be interpreted in ways that reflect the interests and ideologies of its interpreters. Politics can be a crucial part of archaeological interpretation and fuel particular political agendas.[10] Despite the interpretive bias present in archaeology, archaeological evidence can do some things that ancient texts simply cannot. Material artifacts can determine habitation in certain places and time periods and point toward the identity of inhabitants. The material artifacts of the Highland Settlements provide a picture into Israelite history that both enhance and challenge the different presentations of Israelite history that appear in the Bible.

Iron Age I Highland Settlements:
An Archaeological Study

Archaeological research reveals that the Late Bronze Age and early Iron Age in Canaan were periods filled with economic disparity, oppression, and social unrest. Within this social context, the proto-Israelites or Hebrew people emerge onto the historical scene. Who were these people? Where did they come from?[11] These questions have been explored by a variety

---

[10] Andrew Lawler, "Unearthing David's City: Eilat Mazar Dug with a Bible in One Hand and a Spade in the Other. Should Her Theories Be Taken Seriously?," Aeon, December 10, 2021.

[11] This question is drawn from the title of William Dever's book that explores this topic: Dever, *Who Were the Early Israelites and Where Did They Come From?*

of scholars over centuries of research.[12] As discussed above, the Bible tells stories of the Hebrew people that explain who they were and how they came to reside in the land of Canaan.

This chapter discusses the archaeological research from the Late Bronze Age and the early Iron Age in Canaan. The archaeological record, though sparse, still allows for an analysis of what these artifacts can teach about this period and the Highland Settlements. Much can be learned about cultural expression of the Highland Settlements, the wider social and political context of the Egyptian Empire, and the ecological climate during these periods. The second part of the chapter discusses different ways in which biblical scholars interpret the biblical texts alongside the archaeological evidence. Four dominant models of interpreting the Highland Settlements archaeological evidence have emerged during the last seven decades of this developing research. This section examines how scholars make sense of the identity, technology, and cultural practices of the Highland Settlers in conversation with the wider Iron Age context.

Cultural and Ecological Context of the Late Bronze Age in Canaan

What were the social, economic, and ecological contexts of ancient Canaan during the Late Bronze Age, and how did

---

[12]Liverani, *Israel's History and the History of Israel*; Israel Finkelstein and Neil Asher Silberman, *The Bible Unearthed: Archaeology's New Vision of Ancient Israel and the Origin of Its Sacred Texts* (New York: Simon and Schuster, 2002); Dever, *Beyond the Texts*; Dever, *Who Were the Early Israelites and Where Did They Come From?*; McNutt, *Reconstructing the Society of Ancient Israel*; Meyers, *Discovering Eve*; Avraham Faust, *Israel's Ethnogenesis: Settlement, Interaction, Expansion and Resistance*, Approaches to Anthropological Archaeology (London: Equinox, 2006).

these contexts shape the Iron Age I Hebrew Highland Settlements? Scholars identify key pressures in the Late Bronze Age that necessitated a new settlement pattern.

Social Inequality and Unrest

During the late Bronze Age (1350–1250 BCE), Egypt controlled Canaan, ruling through a series of loyal city-states located mostly within its fertile, flat plains.[13] Local client-kings ruled these city-states and were loyal to Egypt. They likely paid some sort of annual tribute or tax, which created an economic burden because many of their goods were given to pay taxes and could not be used for their own subsistence.[14] In return, the local kings expected to receive military support from Egypt to deal with local enemies and to receive grain if supplies ran short.[15] The Late Bronze Age period was filled with socioeconomic tensions created by a stratified social system that led to resource disparities between the urban palace groups and the rural population of local farmers and pastoralists.[16] Archaeological discoveries reveal that, during this time, there existed a cosmopolitan elite ruling class that owned a proliferation of palaces, imported luxury goods, art, writings, and rich tombs.[17] In contrast to the lifestyle of the elite class, around 80 percent of the population lived in villages, grew their own food, and required land for flocks

---

[13]Faust, *Israel's Ethnogenesis*, 160–61.

[14]Volkmar Fritz, *The Emergence of Israel in the 12th and 11th Centuries BCE* (Atlanta: Society of Biblical Literature, 2011), 74. Also see Dever, *Beyond the Texts*, 81.

[15]Liverani, *Israel's History and the History of Israel*, 15; McNutt, *Reconstructing the Society of Ancient Israel*, 45. This system of support from Egypt is attested to in the Amarna letters. See for example (*LA* 154 = *EA* 85).

[16]Liverani, *Israel's History and the History of Israel*, 26.

[17]Dever, *Beyond the Texts*, 78.

of sheep and goats.[18] The wealth inequality created socio-economic tensions in the region, and the rural populations became heavily indebted to the urban ruling class. Farmers often needed to trade material possessions, and even enslave family members, to repay their debts. As a last resort, farmers would either flee to geographically fringe areas or be forced to sell themselves into slavery.[19]

In geographically remote places, away from city-state rule, groups of shepherds, local clans, escaped slaves, and others who had left urban settings converged and coexisted. Some people who fled urban areas were described as *habiru*. The word *habiru* (or *hapiru*, depending on the transliteration) began to appear in Sumerian, Akkadian, Egyptian, and other ancient Near Eastern texts during the second millennium BCE.[20] In these texts, the *habiru* are discussed as "rebels, raiders, soldiers, mercenaries, slaves, outlaws, vagrants, or individuals on the margins of society."[21] Most significant of the ancient texts that reference the *habiru* are the Amarna letters, a collection of Egyptian letters that date from 1360 to

[18]Liverani, *Israel's History and the History of Israel*, 21.

[19]Liverani, *Israel's History and the History of Israel*, 26.

[20]Liverani, *Israel's History and the History of Israel*, 27. Other articles exploring the term *habiru*: Matthew Akers, "What's in a Name? An Examination of the Usage of the Term 'Hebrew' in the Old Testament," *Journal of the Evangelical Theological Society* 55, no. 4 (December 2012): 685–96; Ann E. Killebrew, "Hybridity, Hapiru, and the Archaeology of Ethnicity in Second Millennium BCE Western Asia," in *A Companion to Ethnicity in the Ancient Mediterranean*, ed. Jeremy McInerney (Hoboken, NJ: John Wiley & Sons, 2014), 142–57; Nadav Na'aman, "Habiru and Hebrews: The Transfer of a Social Term to the Literary Sphere," *Journal of Near Eastern Studies* 45, no. 4 (1986): 271–88.

[21]Killebrew, "Hybridity, Hapiru, and the Archaeology of Ethnicity," 146. The diverse texts include Sumerian, Akkadian, Hittite, Mitanni, Ugaritic, and Egyptian sources. *Hapiru* or *'apiru* are other common English transliterations of the term; in cuneiform, the word is SA.GAZ.

1330 BCE. They were written on clay tablets and discovered in Egypt in the late 1800s CE. The Amarna letters contain the written correspondence of Canaanite kings who requested assistance from the pharaoh on local matters in Canaan, and they provide a remarkable glimpse into the socioeconomic conditions of Canaanite cities during the Middle to Late Bronze Ages.[22] In the letters, Canaanite kings wrote to the pharaoh, requesting help to deal with their enemies, like other Canaanite kings they consider traitorous or the *habiru* who were raiding their cities. Egypt did not often intervene in these situations unless actual land was threatened because the Pharaoh's main concern was maintaining control in the region, not appeasing client-kings.[23]

During the Amarna period, the meaning of the term *habiru* changed from meaning "fugitive" to becoming synonymous with "enemy" or "outlaw," and "in some cases, even kings and members of the ruling class were called *habiru* if they were forced to leave their position and flee: this proves the depreciation in the value of the term."[24] Common to the different usages of the term is the idea that *habiru*s had been uprooted from their original contexts and needed to adapt to a new place.[25] Some hypothesize that *habiru* eventually morphed into the word "Hebrew," a move discussed in the sections below.[26]

---

[22]The Amarna letters collection does not contain the pharaoh's response, only the Canaanite kings' requests of the pharaoh. Megan Bishop Moore and Brad E. Kelle, *Biblical History and Israel's Past: The Changing Study of the Bible and History* (Grand Rapids: Eerdmans, 2011), 110. For a complete translation of the Amarna Letters, see William L. Moran, *The Amarna Letters* (Baltimore, MD: Johns Hopkins, 1992).

[23]Liverani, *Israel's History and the History of Israel*, 16.

[24]Liverani, *Israel's History and the History of Israel*, 27.

[25]Naʾaman, "Ḥabiru and Hebrews," 272.

[26]See, for example: Akers, "What's in a Name?"; Killebrew, "Hybridity,

In summary, the Amarna letters show that the Late Bronze Age in Canaan was filled with social turmoil, unrest, and competition between rival city-states. This unrest reached a pinnacle around 1250–1100 BCE when, according to archaeological evidence, the dominant Bronze Age civilizations suffered a major collapse, and Egyptian imperial control of the area began to wane.[27] Furthermore, climate change contributed to this collapse.

Late Bronze Age Climate Change

In addition to social unrest, a dramatic climate change was a likely precipitating factor in the collapse of the Late Bronze Age civilization.[28] Archaeobotanists discovered that widespread climate change occurred during the Late Bronze Age around the Mediterranean by drilling sediment cores from the bottom of the Sea of Galilee and other lakes, studying fossilized pollen trapped in the sediments.[29] The climate change

---

Hapiru, and the Archaeology of Ethnicity"; Na'aman, "Ḥabiru and Hebrews."

[27]Dever, *Beyond the Texts,* 88.

[28]Eric H. Cline, *1177 B.C.: The Year Civilization Collapsed* (Princeton, NJ: Princeton University Press, 2014); Dafna Langgut, Israel Finkelstein, and Thomas Litt, "Climate and the Late Bronze Collapse: New Evidence from the Southern Levant," *Tel Aviv* 40, no. 2 (November 2013): 149–75; Israel Finkelstein and Dafna Langgut, "Dry Climate in the Middle Bronze I and Its Impact on Settlement Patterns in the Levant and Beyond: New Pollen Evidence," *Journal of Near Eastern Studies* 73, no. 2 (2014): 219–34; Alessio Palmisano et al., "Holocene Landscape Dynamics and Long-Term Population Trends in the Levant," *The Holocene* 29, no. 5 (May 1, 2019): 708–27.

[29]Langgut, Finkelstein, and Litt discovered that extreme discrepancies in the amount of pollen contained in different sediment layers indicated years of drought versus years of typical rainfall that occurred at the end of the Bronze Age around the Mediterranean. Here they note that the study of "fossil pollen grains is a powerful tool in the reconstruction of past vegetation and climate history." Langgut, Finkelstein, and Litt, "Climate and the Late Bronze Collapse," 151.

was caused by a warming period that melted several ice sheets in Greenland, shifting weather patterns around the Mediterranean, triggering colder winters and a severe drought (one hundred millimeters [four inches] less rainfall a year) across the Canaanite region for nearly a century.[30] This resulted in the destruction of urban centers, hoarding, and settlement pattern changes.[31] The catastrophic climate shift affected peoples across the Mediterranean and caused mass migrations as people searched for better areas to cultivate food. For example, during this time, Egyptian texts refer to "sea peoples" arriving in the region from across the Mediterranean and assaulting Egyptian-controlled cities for supplies.[32] Under these hostile conditions, Egyptian control of Canaan declined.[33]

The multiple factors of extreme climate change, mass migration, and hostile invasions contributed to the destabilization and eventual collapse of the existing Late Bronze Age civilizations.[34] The Late Bronze Age in Canaan was a tumultuous

---

[30]Langgut, Finkelstein, and Litt, "Climate and the Late Bronze Collapse," 162. Langgut, Finkelstein, and Litt explain that "the driest event throughout the Bronze and Iron Ages occurred 1250–1100 BCE—at the end of the Late Bronze Age. . . . In the Levant the crisis years are represented by destruction of a large number of urban centres, shrinkage of other major sites, hoarding activities and changes in settlement patterns."

[31]Langgut, Finkelstein, and Litt, "Climate and the Late Bronze Collapse," 149.

[32]Cline provides a detailed account of the effects of the invading "sea peoples" on the region in *1177 B.C.: The Year Civilization Collapsed.* Additionally, according to Langgut, Finkelstein, and Litt, this event is illustrated in well-known "accounts of the confrontation between Ramesses III and the Sea Peoples in the dramatic letters found in Ugarit that describe sea-born raids on settlements along the Mediterranean." Langgut, Finkelstein, and Litt, "Climate and the Late Bronze Collapse," 150.

[33]As Liverani observes, "The whole political system of the Late Bronze Age in the eastern Mediterranean collapsed under the assaults of the invaders." Liverani, *Israel's History and the History of Israel*, 35.

[34]As Langgut, Finkelstein, and Litt, explain, "The long-term climatic

period, which created a turbulent chain of events and much human suffering.[35]

Interpretation of Archaeological Evidence

In this difficult context of climate change and the breakdown of the Egyptian-controlled Canaanite city-states, a new settlement pattern began to emerge around 1200 BCE (the beginning of Iron Age I) in the remote highland regions of Canaan.[36] These Highland Settlements mark the beginning of what would later become the Hebrew or Israelite people (in Iron Age II); hence they are often referred to as "proto-Israelite."[37] Most of these settlements were located in previously uninhabited areas.[38] While many of the settlements were located in close proximity to the cities and fertile plains, they were still considered remote because they were situated in rocky and hilly terrain that was difficult to traverse. The chal-

---

changes influenced the stability of the organized kingdoms in the region and led to systemic collapse of the previously well-integrated complex societies in the eastern Mediterranean, depopulation of large areas, urban abandonments and long-distance migration." Langgut, Finkelstein, and Litt, "Climate and the Late Bronze Collapse," 150. See also the table on page 167 that illustrates how these factors affected the entire Mediterranean region.

[35]As Dever explains, "It was not just sites that were destroyed . . . it was people, their lives lost or shattered. Thousands might have been slaughtered, thousands of others made refugees, homeless. The bitter hostility of the writers of the Hebrew Bible, although centuries later, is understandable and probably preserved authentic historical memories." Dever, *Beyond the Texts*, 105.

[36]Faust, *Israel's Ethnogenesis,* 167; Fritz, *The Emergence of Israel,* 82; Liverani, *Israel's History and the History of Israel,* 52; McNutt, *Reconsidering the Society of Ancient Israel,* 48.

[37]Dever, *Who Were the Early Israelites?,* 194; Faust, *Israel's Ethnogenesis,* 167; Fritz, *The Emergence of Israel,* 82; Liverani, *Israel's History and the History of Israel,* 52.

[38]As Volkmar Fritz explains, "The old city centers were usually avoided. . . . The new settlements were predominantly in the mountains and on the margins." Fritz, *The Emergence of Israel,* 82.

lenging topography meant the region was largely uninhabited and off the beaten path. Some settlements were also located in "regions of dense forestation or arid climate and thus were far outside the sphere of influence of the city centers."[39] After 1200 BCE, the number of settlement sites increased fivefold: "In contrast to the limited number of city centers in the Late Bronze Age, the land was covered with a tight network of villages in the Early Iron Age."[40]

Referring to these sites as "proto-Israelite" does not mean that the settlers had a self-conscious Israelite identity. The Israelite identity would not develop until Iron Age II and the monarchic periods.[41] Rather, the term "proto-Israelite" demarks an ongoing process of the development of a new ethnic consciousness. If these earliest settlers did not have an Israelite identity, then who were they?

Who Were the Highland Settlers?

Archaeological artifacts from settlement excavations do not always indicate the inhabitants' cultural and ethnic identities.[42] Nevertheless, material artifacts can provide clues that help determine the cultural characteristics of the population. In the case of the Highland Settlements, these artifacts exhibit significant cultural similarities to the Canaanite city-states,

---

[39]Fritz, *The Emergence of Israel*, 85.

[40]Fritz, *The Emergence of Israel*, 85.

[41]Killebrew, "Hybridity, Hapiru, and the Archaeology of Ethnicity," 151. Here Killebrew notes that most scholars agree that a well-defined Israelite identity would not crystalize until the early first millennium. See also Fritz, *The Emergence of Israel*, 82. Here Fritz explains that "Israel" would not become a self-description of the highland people until the monarchic period. Liverani also explains that new ethnic identity formation is an ongoing developmental process: Liverani, *Israel's History and the History of Israel*, 58–59.

[42]Killebrew explains that "ethnicity is not always clearly signaled or expressed in material culture, complicating efforts to identify peoples archaeologically." Killebrew, "Hybridity, Hapiru, and the Archaeology of Ethnicity," 143.

particularly in pottery styles and cultic elements, like a bull statue found at one of the highland sites.[43] Because of these similarities, a large portion of the settlers were likely indigenous Canaanites, who slowly developed a new cultural pattern during the Iron Age I settlement period.[44] Due to extensive population growth in a relatively short time frame, however, not all of the population can be attributed fully to indigenous Canaanites and natural birth rates.[45]

Scholars hypothesize that the population consisted of a "motley crew" of diverse settlers from around the region, who developed a new pattern of living in the highlands after the collapse of the Bronze Age power centers.[46] Ann E. Killebrew details the complexity of those who constituted this diverse population, including a "rural Canaanite population, displaced peasants and pastoralists, and lawless *hapiru*, as well as semi-nomadic tribes such as the *Shasu*. . . . Fugitive or runaway Semitic slaves from New Kingdom Egypt, a memory of which could be reflected in the exodus account, may have joined this 'mixed multitude.'"[47] Killebrew further explains that the "porous borders" of these small, kin-based groups allowed external groups to join them.[48] Eventually,

---

[43]Dever, *Beyond the Texts*, 178.

[44]See, for example, Liverani, *Israel's History and the History of Israel,* 52; Dever, *Who Were the Ancient Israelites?,* 181. This is explored further in the latter portion of this chapter that discusses models of origins of the Highland Settlements.

[45]Dever, *Beyond the Texts*, 180. Here Dever states that population in the settlement sites was about ten thousand in the thirteenth century, up to forty thousand by the eleventh century. He remarks that this population influx occurred because "there must have been considerable in-migration."

[46]Dever calls the Highland Settlers a "motley crew." See the following sources from Dever for further explanation: Dever, *Who Were the Early Israelites?,* 181; Dever, *Beyond the Texts,* 226–28.

[47]Killebrew, "Hybridity, Hapiru, and the Archaeology of Ethnicity," 151.

[48]Killebrew, "Hybridity, Hapiru, and the Archaeology of Ethnicity," 151–52.

during Iron Age II, this diverse conglomeration of settlers contributed to the ethnogenesis of what would later become known as Israel.[49]

Connections between Habiru and Hebrew

As noted above, some scholars posit a connection between the word *habiru* and the phonetically similar "Hebrew," suggesting that the later term "Hebrew" refers to an ethnic group connected to the nation known as Israel that evolved from the *habiru*, the social outsiders composing part of the settler population in the highlands.[50] Matthew Akers presents a comprehensive history of the term *habiru*, discussing many of the sources where it is used. The term appears in over 210 texts dated from 2500 BCE to 1200 BCE and from places such as Nuzi, Babylonia, Egypt, Sumer, and Arabia, to name only a few.[51] Akers argues, "Evidence abounds that the Hebrews and *Habiru* are related somehow. Perhaps the strongest evidence lies in the words themselves. The consonants that form the words 'Hebrew' and *Habiru* are both *hbr*, rendering the words 'etymologically identical.'"[52] In his view, these terms were etymologically connected, and *habiru* eventually became synonymous with the Hebrew people who descended from Abraham.[53] Not all scholars agree with this connection, however. Anson Rainey refutes any connection between the two terms because *habiru* is a social class, whereas Hebrew is an

---

[49]Fritz, *The Emergence of Israel*, 82; Killebrew, "Hybridity, Hapiru, and the Archaeology of Ethnicity," 151–52.

[50]See Akers, "What's in a Name?"; Killebrew, "Hybridity, Hapiru, and the Archaeology of Ethnicity"; Liverani, *Israel's History and the History of Israel*, 27.

[51]Akers, "What's in a Name?," 687–88.

[52]Akers, "What's in a Name?," 687–88.

[53]Akers, "What's in a Name?," 696.

ethnicon. Rainey regards connecting the two as an example of a certain naiveté among scholars.[54]

Other scholars address the contrasting meanings of the two terms directly. Liverani, like Akers, states that the word *habiru* clearly had "an etymological and semantic connection with most ancient attestations of the term 'Hebrew' (*'ibrî*) before it assumed an ethnic connotation."[55] Similarly, Ann Killebrew argues that it is quite plausible that an evolution of the term *habiru* occurred in which it shifted from a social class designator to an ethnic identifier (that is, from *"Habiru"* to *"Hebrew"*).[56] She explains that ethnicity and social identity are evolving "fluid, contextual, and constructed" processes.[57] Nadav Na'aman shows how the term "Hebrew" evolved through the Hebrew literary tradition, which led to the term becoming equated with "Israelite."[58] Neither ethnicity nor language are fixed. Because they evolve over time, an evolution of the term from *habiru* to "Hebrew" would not be unusual.

Taken as a whole, the evidence suggests that these early settlers were from various backgrounds, cultures, and ethnicities. Over time, the evolving term *habiru* likely became an identity marker or common name that provided unity to this diverse group of peoples. Because the remote geography of the highlands was not directly under the control of the city-state urban centers, the Highland Settlers were able to develop a new settlement pattern that differed from the Late Bronze

---

[54]Anson F. Rainey, "Review of *Habiru-Hebräer, Eine sozio-linguistische Studie über die Herkunft des Gentiliziums 'ibrî; vom Appellativum habiru*, by Oswald Loretz," *Journal of the American Oriental Society* 107, no. 3 (1987): 540–41.

[55]Liverani, *Israel's History and the History of Israel*, 27.

[56]Killebrew, "Hybridity, Hapiru, and the Archaeology of Ethnicity," 143.

[57]Killebrew, "Hybridity, Hapiru, and the Archaeology of Ethnicity," 143.

[58]Na'aman, "Ḥabiru and Hebrews," 288.

Age urban system that was collapsing. The settlement pattern was likely a response both to oppressive socioeconomic conditions and climate changes that led to mass migrations. Over time, common cultural practices emerged across these proto-Israelite settlements, and a common identity and ethnicity began to form that eventually became the nation of Israel.

Technological and Cultural Innovations

Several key features of these Highland Settlements distinguish them as new cultural expressions from the Late Bronze Age Canaanite city-state culture. First, they are rural agricultural and pastoral settlements as opposed to urban. To be successful agro-pastoralists, the people needed to deal with the difficult rocky terrain and drier weather due to the climate change. They addressed such challenges by employing several technological innovations on a broad scale, including terraced agriculture and chalk-lined cisterns. These technologies enabled the settlers to cultivate and inhabit the settlements year-round.[59] Building large terraces backfilled with soil enabled crops to grow in steep, rocky terrain; hewing out chalk-lined cisterns permitted water preservation for use during long dry periods.[60] Neither of these technologies were invented by the settlers; both were developed before the Iron Age. However, the broad employment of these technologies throughout the

---

[59]Sources on terraced agriculture: Dever, *Who Were the Early Israelites?*, 113–14; Dever, *Beyond the Texts*, 176; Liverani, *Israel's History and the History of Israel*, 47; Lawrence E. Stager, "The Archaeology of the Family in Ancient Israel," *Bulletin of the American Schools of Oriental Research* 260 (October 1985): 1–35; Sources on cisterns: Dever, *Who Were the Early Israelites?*, 115–17; Dever, *Beyond the Texts*, 176; Liverani, *Israel's History and the History of Israel*, 47–48; McNutt, *Reconstructing the Society of Ancient Israel*, 50; Stager, "The Archaeology of the Family in Ancient Israel," 9–10.

[60]Dever, *Who Were the Early Israelites?*, 113–17.

Highland Settlements was novel.[61] These technologies converted otherwise untamable lands to arable soil, opening new areas to agriculture.[62]

Another distinguishing innovation of the Highland Settlements was the architectural style of the homes, called the "pillared-house" or "Hebrew house." Although this house form existed at a few other sites in the Late Bronze Age, "the full development of this house form and its ubiquitous adaptation in rural villages *is* new—and it reflects a shift from urban to rural lifestyles."[63] Typical Hebrew houses appeared in nearly all of the settlements and consisted of a basic design, which included four rooms that ran across the back wall, three parallel length-wise work rooms or stables separated by pillars (the center one unroofed), and a second floor with bedrooms.[64] A Hebrew house typically accommodated a nuclear family of five to seven people.[65]

A Highland Settlement often had several Hebrew homes built in a circular or horseshoe pattern, with the exterior walls serving as a protective wall to keep out intruders and wildlife, and to keep in the domestic animals and village children.[66] The

---

[61]As William Dever observes, "It is the *intensification* of the terrace system, and its deployment for sustained agricultural economy that is dependent on it, that is new in Iron I." Dever, *Beyond the Texts*, 176. See also Stager, "The Archaeology of the Family in Ancient Israel," 9–11.

[62]These "strategies were being developed," Paula McNutt explains, so the people could make "the marginal zones in which the villages were situated economically viable by opening up new areas to agriculture." McNutt, *Reconstructing the Society of Ancient Israel*, 50.

[63]Dever, *Beyond the Texts*, 209.

[64]Liverani, *Israel's History and the History of Israel*, 55.

[65]Liverani, *Israel's History and the History of Israel*, 55. The Harvard Museum of the Ancient Near East has a life-size model of a Hebrew house that can be visited in person as well as on their Matterport virtual tour at https://hmane.harvard.edu/. The house was part of *The Houses of Ancient Israel* exhibit, which ran until October 15, 2019.

[66]Fritz explains that "the organization into an enclosed oval is clearly

villages were otherwise unfortified. Some scholars believe that this circular layout follows a pattern similar to what Bedouin peoples use to arrange their tents, suggesting that some of the Highland Settlers might have been Bedouins who sedentarized in the Iron Age I resettlement pattern.[67] A settlement this size would have consisted of around twenty families. During Iron Age I, the proliferation of these small settlement villages was extensive, and more than 250 settlement sites have been identified.[68] Along with the Hebrew house design and village layout, the adoption of "democratizing technologies" and other unique elements set the Highland Settlements apart from Late Bronze Age cultural patterns.

Democratizing Technologies

Some of the technological innovations evidenced in the Highland Settlements archaeological findings are considered "democratizing" because they effectively enabled the small, remote settlements to maintain relative independence from the urban centers.[69] During the Bronze Age, it should not be surprising that bronze was the dominant form of metalwork. The creation of bronze tools required long-distance trade and extensive palace workshops because bronze is a difficult metal to work with and expensive to procure. Iron, on the other hand, is an easier metal to fashion and requires much

---

functionally determined, since it enabled the accommodation of animals as well as serving a certain protective function against attacks." Fritz, *The Emergence of Israel*, 97–98.

[67] For this argument, see Fritz, *The Emergence of Israel*, 98; Liverani, *Israel's History and the History of Israel*, 54.

[68] Liverani, *Israel's History and the History of Israel*, 52.

[69] Avraham Faust, *The Archaeology of Israelite Society in Iron Age II* (Winona Lake, IN: Eisenbrauns, 2012), 222; Faust, *Israel's Ethnogenesis*, 222; Liverani, *Israel's History and the History of Israel*, 45.

simpler tools than bronze-working.[70] The development of iron-working made metal tools accessible to those outside of the palace systems. The socioeconomic collapse at the end of the Bronze Age led to the spread of iron-working because itinerant blacksmiths traveled around producing tools "without need of a palace workshop."[71] In addition, sources of iron were spread across the region and readily available, eliminating the need for complicated and long-distance trading.[72] Several Iron I Highland Settlements show evidence of metalworking, particularly the ability to produce the utilitarian tools needed for agriculture and herding, such as "plow points, knives, goads, and sometimes a steel pick."[73] Ease of use and wide availability led to broader accessibility of metal tools, differing from the Bronze Age in which metal tools were available only to socioeconomic elite classes.[74]

Similarly, the dominant form of writing in the Bronze Age was Babylonian cuneiform, which required an extensive and expensive education and was only accessible to elites.[75] A written alphabet, by contrast, was accessible to much broader groups.[76] Evidence suggests that the Hebrew people began to

---

[70]Liverani, *Israel's History and the History of Israel*, 44–45.

[71]Liverani, *Israel's History and the History of Israel*, 45.

[72]Liverani, *Israel's History and the History of Israel*, 45.

[73]Dever, *Beyond the Texts*, 163, 172.

[74]Liverani, *Israel's History and the History of Israel*, 44–45.

[75]Joshua Berman explains that "in the cultures of the ancient Near East as well as ancient Greece, the production and use of texts was inextricably bound up with the formation of class distinctions: those who possessed the capacity to read and write were members of a trained scribal class who worked in the service of the ruling order." Joshua A. Berman, *Created Equal* (Oxford: Oxford University Press, 2008), 111. For a broad discussion of the topic of writing in ancient Israel, see David Carr, *Writing on the Tablet of the Heart: Origins of Scripture and Literature* (Oxford: Oxford University Press, 2005). See also Liverani, *Israel's History and the History of Israel*, 45.

[76]Berman explains that in contrast to complex administrative languages like

develop an alphabet for Hebrew, part of the Northwest Semitic family of languages that also included Aramaic, Ugaritic, and Phoenician.[77] The early Hebrew people seem to have begun developing this alphabet during Iron Age I, though it would not become prevalent until Iron Age II.[78] After the Late Bronze Age collapse, it began to spread broadly along trade routes in the Mediterranean and Near East.[79] The earliest Hebrew inscription, an ostracon that contains an abecedary that dates to the eleventh century, is an important piece of evidence that attests to early literacy during the Iron I period.[80]

Democratizing innovations in iron-working and the alphabet enabled new sociopolitical groups, like the Highland Settlers, to be relatively independent from the collapsing elite Late Bronze Age palace systems and city-states.[81] Iron-working made the Highland Settlements less dependent on palace systems for much-needed metal tools, and the written

---

Egyptian hieroglyphs or Mesopotamian cuneiform, "The hallmark of the early history of the alphabet, by contrast, is that it was a medium of communication adopted by the lower strata of society and not the state apparatus." Berman, *Created Equal,* 121.

[77] Dever, *Who Were the Early Israelites?*, 200.

[78] Dever, *Who Were the Early Israelites?*, 200; Liverani, *Israel's History and the History of Israel*, 46.

[79] Berman explains that "the spread of writing outside state-sponsored institutions was occasioned in part by the invention of the alphabet. With the advent of the alphabet, it is no surprise that we begin to find inscriptions on potsherds, or ostraca, throughout the southern Levant." Berman, *Created Equal,* 121. See also Liverani, *Israel's History and the History of Israel*, 45.

[80] An ostracon is a broken piece of pottery (potsherd) used for writing. An abecedary is a full alphabet carved into stone or written on another medium used for teaching. Dever, *Who Were the Early Israelites?*, 183.

[81] As Liverani explains, "The [Late Bronze Age] cultural crisis, the emergence of new sociopolitical groups and the new economic opportunities encouraged the adoption of new techniques. And, *vice versa*, the adoption of these new techniques enabled the creation of a new territorial social order." Liverani, *Israel's History and the History of Israel*, 43.

alphabet enabled the Highlands Settlements to record their own texts, law codes, and stories, contributing to the development of their ethnic identity and culture.

In addition to democratizing tools, some groups, including the Highland Settlers, also developed a social system that was less hierarchical and oppressive than the elite palace systems, creating what some call an egalitarian ethos.[82] Material evidence found throughout the Highland Settlements archaeological sites suggests that some sort of egalitarian or nascent democracy was a driving ideology for these practices.[83] The lack of tombs and burial goods throughout the Iron Age is interpreted as evidence of an egalitarian ideology.[84]

The idea that the ancient Israelites practiced some sort of egalitarianism is widely accepted, but that this egalitarian social structure was derived from a unique religious cult (Yahwism) is not. Several decades ago, scholars like George Mendenhall and Norman Gottwald argued that the Highland Settlement egalitarian ethos arose from the Israelite religion.[85]

---

[82]This democratic ethos was not limited to the Highland Settlements; it had precedents in other ancient Near Eastern societies. See Faust, *Israel's Ethnogenesis*, 98–99.

[83]Carol Meyers rejects the term egalitarianism to describe the Highland Settlements. She argues that the term implies an anachronistic sense of equality that did not exist in the Iron Age, and suggests that the term "heterarchy" is a better descriptor, referring to a lateral organizational system where work and roles are spread out among community members and where no steep hierarchies exist between men and women. Carol Meyers, "*Tribes* and Tribulations: Retheorizing Earliest 'Israel'" in *Tracking* The Tribes of Yahweh: *On the Trail of a Classic*, ed. Roland Boer (London: Sheffield Academic, 2002), 42-43.

[84]Faust argues that the Israelite settlements lack any sort of burial system throughout the Iron Age I that differs from other cultures in the area. He concludes that "the answer lies in an ideology of egalitarianism and simplicity. The simplest type of burial is simply a reflection of this ideology or ethos." Avraham Faust, "Early Israel: An Egalitarian Society," *Biblical Archaeology Review* 39, no. 4 (2013): 49.

[85]A central thesis in Norman Gottwald's *Tribes of Yahweh* was that Israelite

This idea was central to Norman Gottwald's arguments in *The Tribes of Yahweh*. Today, however, many, including Gottwald himself, suggest that other sociocultural factors played a role in the formation of an egalitarian ethos, and it was not a nascent Yahwism.[86]

Frank Moore Cross argued that "there is a strong anti-Canaanite, Patriarchal-egalitarian, anti-feudal polemic in early Israel, which appears to be authentic, grounded in history. The [egalitarian] theses of Mendenhall and Gottwald cannot be wholly dismissed."[87] William Dever argues that Gottwald and Mendenhall's thesis revealed "that a socioeconomic revolution was taking place and [they recognized] that the prime movers were part of the indigenous population of Canaan."[88] Faust and others have argued that the Highland Settlements can be "defined as a 'frontier society,' and such societies are very likely to develop an egalitarian ethos."[89] Frontier egalitarian societies can be antagonistic toward the oppressive societies from which they came and can have "populist and democratic ideologies" that acquire a "quasireligious status."[90] Faust ob-

---

egalitarianism arose from the Yahwistic cult. This idea originated with George Mendenhall, Gottwald's teacher, but Gottwald's *Tribes* brought the concept forward in a prominent way. Gottwald has since critiqued his own perspective and no longer interprets the settlements' egalitarianism with regard to Israelite religion, but rather to other social factors.

[86]Faust, *Israel's Ethnogenesis*, 95–107. In a section titled "Israel's Egalitarian Ethos—Summary of Previous Research," Faust provides an excellent discussion of different scholars' view on the topic of an egalitarian ethos of the Highland Settlements.

[87]Frank M. Cross, "Reuben, First-Born of Jacob," *ZAW* 100, Supplement (1988): 62.

[88]Dever, *Beyond the Texts*, 229.

[89]Faust, *Israel's Ethnogenesis*, 104. Others have made this claim as well: See Stager, "The Archaeology of the Family in Ancient Israel," 24–25.

[90]Gerhard Lenski, "*The Tribes of Yahweh: A Sociology of the Religion of Liberated Israel, 1250–1050 B.C.E.* by Norman K. Gottwald," *Religious Studies Review* 6, no. 4 (1980): 275–78.

serves that an egalitarian ethos was not unique to the Highland Settlements; it was a feature of other settlements in the ancient Near East whose inhabitants had left oppressive hierarchical societies.[91] Rather than a frontier society, Dever proposes that the settlements be understood as manifestations of an "agrarian movement with strong reformist tendencies driven by a new social ideal." In many instances, he adds, "[a]grarianism is about more than land; it is *utopian*."[92] According to Mario Liverani, the "Covenant Code" in Exodus 21–23 has a strong "utopian flavor," which he argues should likely be attributed to an early, premonarchic Iron Age I period.[93]

The egalitarian ethos of the Highland Settlements was likely a response to the socioeconomic oppression that frontier settlers had experienced in hierarchical Canaanite societies or from the invading sea peoples, the Philistines.[94] How long did an egalitarian ethos last in the Highland Settlements? Some argue that the Highland Settlements likely exhibited an egalitarian ethos during its initial phases in the Iron Age I period. As a monarchy and nascent state formed during the Iron Age II period, egalitarian praxis began to wane.[95]

An anthropological theory from Victor Turner can help further elucidate the Highland Settlements pattern at the collapse of the Bronze Age as part of a common, cross-cultural social pattern. Turner hypothesizes that societal organizing follows a common pattern of change in which societies move in a spiraling rhythm of structure, anti-structure, and what he terms

---

[91]Faust, *Israel's Ethnogenesis*, 98–99. Here Faust describes other Near Eastern settlements that likely contained egalitarian social structures.

[92]Dever, *Beyond the Texts*, 249, italics added.

[93]Liverani, *Israel's History and the History of Israel*, 67–68.

[94]Faust, *Israel's Ethnogenesis*, 95–107.

[95]Faust, *Israel's Ethnogenesis*, 104–7.

communitas. For Turner, structure describes an established, institutionalized society. Eventually, such a society ceases to function well, often oppressing or marginalizing some people within the society. Turner describes this dysfunction as anti-structure. Social movements that emerge from the margins of anti-structure or dysfunctional societies create new and more egalitarian societies characterized by communitas. As the society responds to new factors in its world and communitas movements become larger and more established, they tend to enter institutional phases of life, becoming the next structure.

Turner's typology is useful in understanding the changing societal structure of the Highland Settlements, beginning by leaving oppressive Canaanite cities, then establishing egalitarian and agrarian settlements, and, lastly, moving toward a monarchic state. Using Turner's typology, the Highland Settlements can be interpreted as a communitas movement emerging on the fringes of the Late Bronze Age structure. By the time of Iron Age II and the rise of the monarchy and Israelite state, they have entered into a structured phase.

While the Highland Settlements moved toward a more hierarchal, structured phase, the egalitarian ethos of the communitas phase was not fully lost, and the memory of an egalitarian past was preserved, in part, in biblical texts. Because egalitarian traditions persisted many years after the Iron Age I settlements, the egalitarian ethos seems to have been important to Israelite self-identity.

> Even if all the [biblical] textual evidence is no more than "propaganda," its very existence proves that there was an audience for it. Its purpose as a mere justification or an effort to disguise actuality would still indicate that such a cover-up was needed—that people "demanded"

it. This by itself indicates that an egalitarian ethos of a sort existed in ancient Israel.[96]

Even though the biblical texts were written well after the egalitarian communitas phase of the Iron Age I settlements, many texts preserved aspects of this earlier time. To be sure, an egalitarian ethos is not the only ideology attested to in the Bible. Hierarchical and even imperial ideologies also pervade many of the biblical texts, standing in stark contrast to what archaeological evidence reveals about the Highland Settlements and the origins of the Hebrew people. However, the memory of the Highland Settlements is an egalitarian specter that haunts these later hierarchical traditions.

The discussion of the democratization and egalitarianism of the Highland Settlements leads to other cultural questions, such as what role (if any) did religion have in shaping the ideology of the settlements. The following section examines how certain archaeological evidence aligns with and contradicts particular biblical texts. The section also discusses four prominent interpretive models of the Highland Settlements materials advanced by biblical scholars and archaeologists.

The Religion and Ideology of the Highland Settlements

A notable characteristic of the Iron Age I Highland Settlements is that, unlike Canaanite city-states, they did not contain

---

[96]Faust, *Israel's Ethnogenesis*, 105. Dever makes a similar argument when he argues that the more egalitarian and patrimonial social organization of the early settlements is preserved in the Bible: "The later biblical writers downplay the sociology of Israel's beginning, but it is nevertheless evident in the theology that they preserved. While some may see their work simply as a later rationalization, we may regard it more realistically as part of an authentic folk memory (i.e., cultural memory)." Dever, *Beyond the Texts*, 228.

prominent cultic structures or temples.[97] Paula McNutt notes, "There is very little material evidence relating to religious practice in Iron Age I highland sites."[98] Avraham Faust explains that "the lack of cultic buildings is an important feature of Israelite religion."[99] Rare exceptions are an open-air cultic complex known as the "Bull Site" at Mount Ebal, where a shrine with a bull statue was found, and another shrine uncovered in a village area.[100] Dever notes that the statue found at the Bull Site is almost identical to one unearthed in the Late Bronze Age Canaanite city of Hazor. He argues, therefore, that "the old Canaanite belief system still prevailed."[101] Dever further states that the sparse evidence points to a carry-over from the Late Bronze Canaanite cult: "We now know that Israelite folk or family religion (and even organized religion)

---

[97]Avraham Faust, "Israelite Temples: Where Was Israelite Cult Not Practiced and Why," *Religions* 10, no. 2 (February 12, 2019): 106. See also Avraham Faust, *The Archaeology of Israelite Society in Iron Age II* (Winona Lake: Eisenbrauns, 2012), 242–43; Zev Farber, "Religion in Eighth-Century Judah: An Overview," in *Archaeology and History of Eighth-Century Judah*, ed. Zev I. Farber and Jacob L. Wright (Atlanta: Society of Biblical Literature, 2018), 431–53. Carol Meyers also discusses how household rituals were the dominant form of ritual practice by most ancient Israelites as temple complexes were rare. See Carol Meyers, "Contributing to Continuity: Women and Sacrifice in Ancient Israel," in *Women, Religion, and the Gift: An Abundance of Riches*, ed. Morny Joy, Sophia Studies in Cross-Cultural Philosophy of Traditions and Cultures 17 (Cham: Springer, 2017), 11.

[98]McNutt, *Reconstructing the Society of Ancient Israel*, 51. A. Mazor concurs: "Archaeological evidence for Israelite cult practices during the settlement period is meager." Amaihai Mazor, "The Iron Age I," in *Archaeology in Ancient Israel*, ed. Amnon Ben-Tor (New Haven, CT: Yale University Press, 1992), 298.

[99]Faust explains that the lack of cultic structures "stands in stark contrast to the way the Canaanite religions were practiced in the Bronze Age, and also to the religious practices in other Iron Age polities and to some extent even by non-Israelites in the kingdoms of Israel and Judah . . . but appears to be a key to understanding Israelite religious practices." Faust, "Israelite Temples."

[100]Liverani, *Israel's History and the History of Israel*, 58.

[101]Dever, *Beyond the Texts*, 178.

were [*sic*] characterized by many of the same older Canaanite features from start to finish."[102]

This cultic archaeological evidence seems to contradict biblical stories that depict the early Israelites as practitioners of a Yahwistic cult. As McNutt observes, archaeological evidence from this period does not tell "us anything about whether or to what extent the worship of the god Yahweh played any part in the processes that occurred in the transition from Late Bronze Age to Iron Age I Palestine."[103] The lack of Yahwistic evidence leads Mario Liverani to conclude, "The social ferment at the base of the 'new society' does not seem to exhibit the religious flavor that the later historiography [in the Bible] attributes to it . . . unless it was a religious movement opposed to any large-scale cultic structure."[104] Similarly, Volkmar Fritz confirms, "Because of the paucity of sources, the theological significance of the era can no longer be ascertained. . . . Religious practices and convictions remain unknown."[105] What little evidence there is, like the Bull Site, points toward a continuation of Late Bronze Age Canaanite religion, suggesting that an overt form of Yahwism was absent from these early Iron Age I Highland Settlements.

Religion is often a source of ideology for groups, but, in the case of Iron I settlements, evidence directly connected to cultic practice is lacking. Some scholars contend that this lack of evidence itself reveals an ideology. In particular, the lack of temples, other hierarchical structures, and tombs during the Iron Age I period indicates an egalitarian ethos or ideology. According to Avraham Faust, a lack of hierarchical

---

[102]Dever, *Beyond the Texts*, 216.

[103]McNutt, *Reconstructing the Society of Ancient Israel*, 51.

[104]Liverani, *Israel's History and the History of Israel*, 58.

[105]Fritz, *The Emergence of Israel*, 241.

structures signals this underlying ideology: "Religion is an important factor that can be used to enhance ethnicity, and the absence of temples could have been used to send a message of difference in regard to both Canaanite and Philistine societies. For our purposes, the lack of elaborated cult is also of importance for the identification of an egalitarian ethos."[106] Faust suggests that the lack of monumental religious structures may indicate a form of egalitarianism, a way of distinguishing the Highland Settlements from hierarchical societies that surrounded them.[107]

The Bible and Archaeology: Contradiction and Congruence

The archaeological record and the biblical record are significant sources of history for the origins of the Hebrew people in Canaan. The Bible, though, contains multiple histories, with many frequently contradicting each other, some contradicting the archaeological evidence from the Highland Settlements, and still others in congruence with the archaeological record. This section briefly surveys some of these texts.

Biblical archaeologists began research in Israel and Palestine in order to discover evidence of Israelite history as it is told in the Bible, but what they found at times contradicts the biblical stories.[108] For example, archaeological evidence

---

[106]Faust, *Israel's Ethnogenesis*, 94; Dever, *Beyond the Texts*, 223. Paula McNutt also makes a similar point to Faust and notes that a *lack* of elaborate structures, which is homogeneous throughout the Iron Age I Highland Settlements, "suggests a relative absence of specialized elites, as is also indicated by the absence of monumental and public structures." McNutt, *Reconstructing the Society of Ancient Israel*, 48.

[107]Faust, "Israelite Temples," 15.

[108]Early archaeologists like William Albright searched for evidence of the

shows no evidence of an Israelite conquest or occupation of Late Bronze Age sites mentioned in the book of Joshua conquest account (e.g., Jericho, Ai, and Gibeon in Joshua 2–9). Indeed, the Egyptian Empire maintained control over Canaan during the Late Bronze period, when the Israelite conquest supposedly occurred.[109] While some signs of destruction are evident at these cities, they cannot "be attributed with any confidence to a group of people called Israelites, led by an individual hero named Joshua."[110] Furthermore, while some cities mentioned in the Bible, like Hormah, Arad, Jericho, and Ai did in fact suffer violent destructions, these occurred during the Early Bronze Age, and they were mostly unoccupied when the Israelites' conquest supposedly occurred in the Late Bronze Age.[111] The archaeological evidence does not support the biblical narrative that an Israelite conquest of Canaanite cities took place in the Late Bronze Age as the Bible reports; many of the cities were not even occupied at the time of the supposed conquest.[112]

---

histories told in the Bible within the archaeological record in order to prove the accuracy of the text. However, "the Bible-as-guidebook approach fell from favour among academics long ago. Excavators today are generally less enamoured of unearthing royal tombs and ancient shrines than with determining what people ate, with whom they traded, and how their material culture changed over time." Lawler, "Unearthing David's City."

[109]Donald B. Redford, *Egypt, Canaan, and Israel in Ancient Times* (Princeton, NJ: Princeton University Press, 1993), 264.

[110]McNutt, *Reconstructing the Society of Ancient Israel*, 54.

[111]Redford, *Egypt, Canaan, and Israel*, 264.

[112]The lack of evidence of a biblical conquest raises questions. Paula McNutt asks, "Why, if the early Israelites were outsiders who came in and destroyed the Canaanites, there is such strong evidence of cultural continuity with Late Bronze Age Canaanite culture?" McNutt, *Reconstructing the Society of Ancient Israel*, 66. However, some scholars still adhere to the historicity of the conquest narrative in the Bible, even if they admit that the stories are hyperbolic. See Hélène M. Dallaire, "Taking the Land by Force," in *Wrestling with the Violence of God: Soundings in the Old Testament*, ed. M. Daniel Carroll

In another example, the biblical texts contradict one another regarding the conquest story and the killing of the native inhabitants of Canaan. The conquest narrative in Joshua tells that Israelites destroyed many Canaanite cities, killing all of the inhabitants because God ordered the Israelites to place them under the *ḥerem*, or ban (Josh 6:21). However, several passages in the book of Judges contradict this story, acknowledging that the Israelite tribes were unable to expel or destroy the indigenous inhabitants and, as a result, settled alongside them. These three examples are illustrative:

> The Lord was with Judah, and he took possession of the hill country, but he could not drive out the inhabitants of the plain, because they had chariots of iron. (Judg 1:19)
> But the Benjaminites did not drive out the Jebusites who lived in Jerusalem; so the Jebusites have lived in Jerusalem among the Benjaminites to this day. (Judg 1:21)
> Manasseh did not drive out the inhabitants of Bethshean and its villages, or Taanach and its villages, or the inhabitants of Dor and its villages, or the inhabitants of Ibleam and its villages, or the inhabitants of Megiddo and its villages; but the Canaanites continued to live in that land. When Israel grew strong, they put the Canaanites to forced labor, but did not in fact drive them out. (Judg 1:27–28)

The book of Judges explains why the Canaanites continued in the land even after they were supposedly destroyed in the *ḥerem* of Joshua's conquest:

R. and J. Willgus, Bulletin for Biblical Research Supplement 10 (University Park: Penn State University Press, 2015), 72.

Now the angel of the LORD went up from Gilgal to Bochim, and said, "I brought you up from Egypt, and brought you into the land that I had promised to your ancestors. I said, 'I will never break my covenant with you. For your part, do not make a covenant with the inhabitants of this land; tear down their altars.' But you have not obeyed my command. See what you have done! So now I say, 'I will not drive them out before you; but they shall become adversaries to you, and their gods shall be a snare to you.'" (Judg 2:1–3)

According to this explanation, the Canaanites remained in the land because the Israelites did not obey Yahweh's command to tear down the altars of the Canaanites.

Lastly, the book of Judges describes early Israelite culture through stories about everyday life that coincide with archaeological data from the Highland Settlements.[113] The "archaeological material from the Iron Age villages provides an assemblage of material culture that seems to agree in some respects with the social conditions implied in Judges and Samuel."[114] In this case, the book of Judges provides glimpses into the Highland Settlements era.[115]

As these examples attest, the Bible does not speak consistently about Israel's origins in Canaan. While some archaeological data stand in stark contrast with certain biblical narratives, including the conquest narrative, other texts, such as Judges, are strikingly similar. These differing accounts require biblical scholars to synthesize archaeological evidence with biblical traditions, and they have done so in a variety of ways.

---

[113]Dever, *Beyond the Texts*, 188.

[114]McNutt, *Reconstructing the Society of Ancient Israel*, 66.

[115]Norman Gottwald explains that "the biblical traditions about pre-state Israel provide 'glimpses' and 'echoes' of a people among whom social power was broadly distributed in local settings." Gottwald, *Politics of Ancient Israel*, 170.

Exodus as Highland Settlements Memory

Several biblical scholars draw a connection between the exodus story and the Highland Settlements. William H. C. Propp speculates that the biblical exodus story could be a conflation of a broad set of Israelite experiences that does not represent one specific experience of the Israelites but rather represents their collective experience.[116] Ron Hendel finds a similar correlation between the exodus story and the Highland Settlements through a cultural memory approach to history known as "mnemohistory," which explores how the past is used to construct a collective identity within the present and also how past events are remembered through a conglomeration of what is historically true and what is remembered symbolically.[117]

Using a mnemohistory approach, Hendel argues that Egyptian imperialism in Canaan from the Early to Late Bronze Age (350 years) was economically oppressive with a widespread slave trade and servitude. The oppression of the Canaanite people during the Bronze Age Egyptian rule could have cultivated a cultural memory of enslavement across generations. From Hendel's perspective, the exodus story can be understood as a symbolic story for the *collective* Canaanite people that narrates the common oppression they suffered under Egyptian imperialism during the Bronze and early Iron Ages rather than the experience of one specific group of people as told in the

---

[116]William H. C. Propp, *Exodus 19–40: A New Translation with Introduction and Commentary* (New York: Doubleday, 2006), 741.

[117]Ronald Hendel, *Remembering Abraham* (New York: Oxford University Press, 2005), 70. Similar to feminist and other critical theorist approaches to history, mnemohistory examines how the historically true and the symbolic are interwoven into historical memory in such a way that the past can authorize the present (70). Mnemohistory explores texts, artifacts, and other cultural discourses to understand how they construct some particular histories, and how these histories "serve to inform and influence the cultural present" (58–59).

Bible. Hendel contends that many aspects of the biblical exodus story, including the unnamed pharaoh, function as an open-ended symbol that represents the experience of a broad swath of the Canaanite population across the settlement time period.[118] The Canaanite experience of oppression likely led the Highland Settlers to form a collective identity as former victims of the Egyptian regime since memories of shared suffering can be a catalyzing factor in the development of ethnic identities.[119] For Hendel, the exodus story created a sense of collective identity that would eventually lead to a distinct Israelite ethnicity.

Following Hendel, Nadav Na'aman speculates that the exodus story may be the earliest source for understanding the cultural and religious worldview of the ancient Israelites.[120] He, too, argues that the basic plot of Exodus represents the cultural memory of the Canaanites who experienced the sudden withdrawal of Egypt from Canaan at the end of the Late Bronze Age after nearly 350 years of subjugation. Egypt's departure from Canaan would have meant freedom and liberation for the Canaanite people who lived under imperial oppression for centuries. Na'aman argues that eventually the cultural memory of Egypt miraculously leaving Canaan was inverted or flipped in the biblical exodus story and the main

---

[118]Ronald Hendel, *Remembering Abraham*, 60–62. Here Hendel explains that "by leaving the name of Pharaoh a blank, the memory of Egyptian oppression could extend to all who had felt the oppression of Pharaoh at any time in the remembered past. This extension of reference extends broadly throughout Canaan during the Egyptian Empire of the Late Bronze Age."

[119]Ronald Hendel, *Remembering Abraham*, 62.

[120]Na'aman also uses a cultural memory studies approach to interpreting the Exodus story. Nadav Na'aman, "Out of Egypt or Out of Canaan? The Exodus Story between Memory and Historical Reality," in *Israel's Exodus in Transdisciplinary Perspective: Text, Archaeology, Culture, and Geoscience*, ed. Thomas E. Levy, Thomas Schneider, and William H. C. Propp (Cham: Springer International, 2015), 531.

plot became the Israelites leaving Egypt. Mario Liverani argues a similar point, suggesting that the exodus story reflects the shift in sovereignty when Egypt left Canaan without reflecting the movement of the Canaanites.[121]

However, no such literary flip would have been needed because Egypt's departure from Canaan was not the only movement occurring during the Late Bronze Age and Early Iron Age periods. Many indigenous Canaanites were also on the move. Migrating Canaanites left or came out of Egypt as they chose to move away from Egyptian-controlled city-states and begin a new settlement pattern in the highlands. While Egypt in the biblical story of Exodus is equated to Egypt as we geographically understand it today, a Late Bronze Age understanding of the Egyptian Empire could have included Canaan as part of Egypt. With this broader geographic and imperial understanding of Egypt, the Highland Settlers did leave Egypt, so to speak. The biblical version of the Exodus collapses the broader understanding of Egypt and makes the events of the exodus much more specific, concrete, and literal. The written story loses the wider meta-experience of various Canaanite people fleeing Egypt from various places and resettling in the highlands, becoming a macro-story narrating the broader cultural memory in a specific way.

As these interpretive works of Hendel and Na'aman attest, the Highland Settlements can be an important interpretive interlocutor for intuiting a broader understanding of the exodus story. More detail will be provided on this topic in chapter 4.

---

[121]Mario Liverani, *Prestige and Interest: International Relations in the Near East ca. 1600–1100 B.C.* (Padova: Sargon SRL, 1990), 277–82. Here, to formulate his hypothesis, Liverani looks at certain Hebrew verb forms that were synonymous with liberation and freedom but did not indicate movement.

Interpretations of Israelite Origins in Canaan

The Bible aligns with archaeological research at times. In other texts, it does not. In the examples of Judges and Exodus, the Bible congruently captures the essence of the Highland Settlements period. In contrast, the archaeological record challenges the biblical texts of an Israelite conquest. Over the last century, four prominent interpretive frames for understanding Israel's origins in the land of Canaan have sought to resolve tensions between biblical texts and archaeology. The frameworks have changed as more archaeological evidence was discovered and scholars with different ideological or religious perspectives interpreted the material. The four most prominent frames of interpretation are the conquest theory, the peaceful infiltration theory, the peasant revolt theory, and the indigenous origins theory.

Conquest Theory

Around the mid-twentieth century, William Foxwell Albright and his students, J. Bright and G. E. Wright, working from a conviction that the Bible was historically accurate, developed what is known as the conquest theory, which argued that the book of Joshua was historically sound.[122] To support their argument, they drew on evidence that seemed to match the date of destruction of several Bronze Age cities with the supposed date of the biblical conquest account.[123] Until the

---

[122]McNutt, *Reconstructing the Society of Ancient Israel*, 53; Moore and Kelle, *Biblical History and Israel's Past*, 14.

[123]See, for example, William Foxwell Albright, "Archaeology and the Date of the Hebrew Conquest of Palestine," *Bulletin of the American Schools of Oriental Research* 58 (1935): 10–18; Albright, "The Israelite Conquest of

1960s, archaeologists dated the destruction of cities such as Bethel, Lachish, and Hazor to the late thirteenth to early twelfth centuries BCE.[124] Albright attributed the destruction of these cities to the Israelites, giving the biblical text the historical "benefit of doubt."[125] The development of better dating techniques after the 1960s challenged the conquest theory by no longer dating the destruction of these cities to the early Iron Age, as previously thought. Without correlative dates of destruction between these cities and an Iron Age Israelite conquest, there was no longer archaeological evidence to support the biblical conquest, thus undermining Albright, Bright, and Wright's conquest theory.

However, despite the lack of corroborating archaeological evidence of an Israelite conquest, some argue that the militaristic account of Israelite origins is still plausible even if it is not exactly how the Bible portrays it. Iain Provan, V. Philips Long, and Tremper Longman III argue in *A Biblical History of Israel* that the truthfulness of scriptural texts should be given the benefit of the doubt, and that the biblical writers should be trusted to capture the essence of Israelite history even if it was done in an artful form.[126] Their interpretive approach prioritizes the historical testimony of biblical texts themselves and discounts other theories that challenge the accuracy of the biblical narratives. The authors argue that when "text and artifact are read properly," that is, as they interpret them, then archaeology does not invalidate any biblical text.[127] However,

---

Canaan in the Light of Archaeology," *Bulletin of the American Schools of Oriental Research* 74 (1939): 11–23.

[124]Dever, *Who Were the Early Israelites?*, 44.

[125]Dever, *Who Were the Early Israelites?*, 44.

[126]Iain W. Provan, V. Philips Long, and Tremper Longman III, *A Biblical History of Israel*, 2nd ed. (Louisville, KY: Westminster John Knox, 2015), 88.

[127]Provan, Long, and Longman III, *A Biblical History of Israel*, 258.

their interpretation of the archaeological evidence is dependent upon challenging the dating of destruction at sites like Jericho (they note the partial and changing nature of archaeology). For these authors, Joshua attests to Israel's initial conquest of Canaan, and the book of Judges chronicles a period of faithlessness of the Israelites indicated by their "Canaanization" evidenced in stories throughout Judges.[128] The book does not engage historical-critical research that discusses the book of Joshua in relation to a seventh-century Deuteronomistic History and the sociopolitical aims of these later Deuteronomist authors, which will be discussed in Chapter 3. Instead, *A Biblical History of Israel* assumes an earlier dating of Joshua and its historical, albeit artful, description of the Israelite past.

Similarly, Héléne Dallaire also prioritizes the historicity of the biblical account while admitting that it is hyperbolic.[129] She argues that Joshua should be read not "as an exact description of the events but rather as historical national literature in which the accounts reflect the literary traditions of the day, the rhetoric of military records, and the theological language of Israel."[130] A protracted military conquest could have occurred during the early Iron Age even if it was much smaller than the Bible attests. She does engage with theories of a Deuteronomistic authorship of Joshua but refutes the notion that the conquest narrative represents an ideological projection from the time of Josiah. The biblical writers, then, could have developed their militaristic story from the time of the Hittites or Egyptians from the Iron Age.

However, Dallaire does not engage the Highland Settlements history and how it contradicts a militaristic conquest, focusing only on whether the conquest text supports some sort

---

[128]Provan, Long, and Longman III, *A Biblical History of Israel*, 258.
[129]Dallaire, "Taking the Land by Force," 59.
[130]Dallaire, "Taking the Land by Force," 72.

of historical conquest. She does not discuss the data that the Highland Settlements were not militaristic or that they were largely indigenous Canaanites themselves. For Dallaire, the Israelites originated outside of Canaan and God helped them to establish themselves in the Land of Canaan in an effort to avoid the immorality of the Canaanites. From this standpoint, her argument for an Iron Age conquest lacks engagement with key details of the Highland Settlements.

Peaceful Infiltration Theory

In contrast to the conquest theory, the peaceful infiltration interpretive framework, developed by Albrecht Alt and supported by Martin Noth and Manfred Weippert, proposed that the Highland Settlements were created peacefully by the sedentarization of pastoral nomads who infiltrated Canaan from the outside.[131] Alt used sociological ethnographic research of twentieth-century Middle Eastern nomads to develop his theory. Showing how many nomads eventually "settled down to become peasant farmers or towns people," these studies led Alt to propose that settling nomads were the Iron Age I Highland Settlers.[132] Israel Finklestein later built on the idea of settling nomads by arguing that the circular arrangement of Hebrew houses in the Highland Settlements mimics Bedouin encampments that can also be arranged in a circular pattern to create an outer defense wall.[133]

---

[131] See Albrecht Alt, *Essays on Old Testament History and Religion* (Oxford: Blackwell, 1966), 133–69; Martin Noth, *The History of Israel* (London: A&C Black, 1958), 53–84; Manfred Weippert, "The Settlement of the Israelite Tribes in Palestine: A Critical Survey of Recent Scholarly Debate," *Studies in Biblical Theology 2* (London: SCM, 1971).

[132] Dever, *Who Were the Early Israelites?*, 50.

[133] See Israel Finkelstein, *The Archaeology of the Israelite Settlement* (Jerusalem: Israel Exploration Society, 1988).

Like the conquest theory, the peaceful infiltration theory was influenced by the Bible, though not in such a literal way as the conquest theory. Moore and Kelle explain that the "Altian" or peaceful infiltration theory of interpretation does not accept biblical history at face value, but finds useful historical information in the Bible's core traditions.[134] They based their theory on the idea that Judges 1 represents a more accurate version of Israelite settlement in Canaan as it coincides with the sedentarization of pastoral nomads from other regions into Canaan, intermingling with and marrying into the indigenous Canaanites.[135] The ethnographic parallels of twentieth-century Bedouins with biblical stories (like those in Judges) led to the popularity of the peaceful infiltration frame of interpretation for several decades in the mid-twentieth century.[136]

Like the conquest theory, developing research methods also brought challenges to the peaceful infiltration theory. First, the sociological methods used to study the Bedouins in the early twentieth century were found to be superficial and heavily influenced by colonial European misconceptions of the Middle East.[137] Second, there were far more people inhabiting the Iron Age I Highland Settlements than there were nomads in the region, so the settlers could not all have been sedentarized nomads.[138] Third, many cultural artifacts found in the settlements were of Canaanite origin and indicate a largely indigenous population that could not have comprised largely nomadic people from outside of Canaan.[139] Despite these critiques, the peaceful infiltration theory influenced developing frames of interpretation in the 1970s.

---

[134]Moore and Kelle, *Biblical History and Israel's Past*, 16–17.

[135]McNutt, *Reconstructing the Society of Ancient Israel*, 54.

[136]Dever, *Who Were the Early Israelites?*, 51.

[137]Dever, *Who Were the Early Israelites?*, 52.

[138]Dever, *Beyond the Texts*, 199–201.

[139]Dever, *Beyond the Texts*, 199–201.

Peasant Revolt or Withdrawal Theory

A third theory—the peasant revolt or withdrawal theory—proposes that the bulk of the Highland Settlers were among local Canaanite populations that revolted against socioeconomic oppression in the Canaanite city-state system and relocated to the remote highlands regions.[140] Hence, most of the highland population consisted of indigenous Canaanites, not outsiders, as the Bible suggests. George Mendenhall put forward this theory, arguing that the Amarna letters and the biblical stories "represent the same process: namely, the withdrawal, not physically and geographically, but politically and subjectively, of large population groups from any obligation to the existing political regimes, and therefore, the renunciation of any protection from those sources."[141] Mendenhall's student Norman Gottwald later expanded, modified, and popularized this theory in his 1979 book, *The Tribes of Yahweh*.[142]

Gottwald was driven to write *Tribes* by a desire to understand from where the Hebrew prophets derived their passionate political perspectives, asking what "traditions and memories informed them."[143] Gottwald concluded that neither the Bible nor biblical scholarship provided plausible answers to his question, so he turned to social theory and anthropology, cultivating a theory of peasant revolt.[144] Using a Marxist analysis, Gottwald argued that economic and social situations triggered the revolt. His interpretation differed from that of Mendenhall, who argued that the social change was driven primarily by

---

[140]McNutt, *Reconstructing the Society of Ancient Israel*, 54–55.

[141]George F. Mendenhall, "The Hebrew Conquest of Palestine," *Biblical Archaeologist* 25, no. 3 (1962): 73.

[142]Gottwald, *The Tribes of Yahweh*.

[143]Gottwald, "Political Activism and Biblical Scholarship: An Interview," in *Tracking* The Tribes of Yahweh, 162–63.

[144]Gottwald, "Political Activism and Biblical Scholarship," 162–63.

Yahwistic religious ideology. Like Mendenhall, however, he emphasized that Yahwism played a prominent role in shaping the ideology that led to revolt. Gottwald later abandoned this idea as archaeologists found no evidence of a Yahwistic cult in the early settlements. He concluded, "We cannot assume pan-Israelite unanimity in devotion to Yahweh."[145]

Gottwald's description of ancient Israel as egalitarian has been critiqued as being anachronistic, and he has since revised his description in naming the organizational structure of ancient Israel as communitarian.[146] Carol Meyers explains that egalitarianism implies an anachronistic sense of equality that did not exist in the Iron Age.[147] She suggests that the term "heterarchy" is a better descriptor, referring to a lateral organizational system where work and roles are spread out among community members and no steep hierarchies exist between men and women.[148]

Meyers argues that, like egalitarianism, patriarchy is a concept that is often used anachronistically to interpret ancient modes of social organization. Patriarchy is often employed to indicate a societal construction in which women are completely dominated by men and have no shared power. She argues that patriarchy is a modernist sociological construct that emerged during the mid-nineteenth century in certain legal,

---

[145]Gottwald, "Response to Contributors," in *Tracking* The Tribes of Yahweh, 176.

[146]Norman K. Gottwald, "Social Class as an Analytic and Hermeneutical Category in Biblical Studies," *Journal of Biblical Literature* 112, no. 1 (1993): 7.

[147]See Carol L. Meyers, "Review: Reconstructing the Society of Ancient Israel," *Bulletin of the American Schools of Oriental Research* 230 (2000): 95–96; Carol Meyers, "*Tribes* and Tribulations: Retheorizing Earliest 'Israel,'" in *Tracking* The Tribes of Yahweh, 42–43; Carol Meyers, "Was Ancient Israel a Patriarchal Society?," *Journal of Biblical Literature* 133, no. 1 (2014): 8–27.

[148]Meyers, "*Tribes* and Tribulations," 42–43.

classics, anthropological, and biblical studies texts.[149] Patriarchy does not accurately characterize the social organization of proto-Israelite settlements, but is rather a simplistic designation that does not depict the complexities of the household and social organizational patterns.[150] Heterarchy, by contrast, recognizes that women and men controlled specific, different, laterally organized domains in society.[151] Heterarchical systems distribute power and social ranking laterally, rather than strictly vertically. Meyers's work shows that, even though the early settlements were not fully egalitarian, as some scholars have speculated, they were far more equitable than oppressive, hierarchical social systems. In later revisions of his own theory, Gottwald has agreed with Meyers's heterarchical description of the Highland Settlements.[152]

---

[149]She traces the genealogy of the term patriarchy here: Meyers, "Was Ancient Israel a Patriarchal Society?," 9–16.

[150]As Meyers explains, "Recovering the household context of women's lives [in ancient Israel] also means challenging the validity of *patriarchy* as a designation for Israelite society. Facile use of that model not only contributes to the negative stereotypes about women in the period of the Hebrew Bible, but also is less accurate than *heterarchy* in depicting the complexities of household life and general sociopolitical organization in the Israelite past." Carol L. Meyers, *Rediscovering Eve: Ancient Israelite Women in Context* (New York: Oxford University Press, 2013), 202.

[151]Here Meyers develops Crumley's argument, describing how the elements of heterarchy are different from a strictly hierarchical social organization: "Elements in hierarchical structure are frequently perceived as being vertical . . . whereas heterarchical structure is most easily envisioned as lateral. . . . The heterarchic model removes the tendency to privilege stratification and ranking as the hallmark of a complex society. . . . Rather, a multiplicity of systems means that a social unit, even an individual, can rank simultaneously high in one modality and low in another. Further, some rankings, such as those linked to age, are fluid and would vary over time." Meyers, "*Tribes* and Tribulations," in *Tracking* The Tribes of Yahweh, 42–43.

[152]Norman K. Gottwald, "Revisiting *The Tribes of Yahweh*," *Servicios Koinonia: Servicio Biblico Latinoamericano* 374, http://servicioskoinonia. org/relat/374e.htm.

Despite Meyers's critique, "egalitarian" has remained a prominent descriptor in some archaeological and biblical studies discourses. Although I, too, use the term "egalitarian" at times, especially in dialogue with this discourse, I do so with the nuanced understanding of heterarchy that Meyers proposes. In addition to using the term "heterarchy" rather than "patriarchy" to describe the proto-Israelite settlements, other refinements of the peasant revolt or withdrawal framework have led to the introduction of new theories.

Indigenous Origins Theory

The indigenous origins theory is a broad framework that has been inspired by and emerged from critiques of the peasant revolt theory. Similar to the peasant revolt theory, indigenous origins emphasizes that the Highland Settlers consisted largely of indigenous Canaanites who withdrew from the urban city-states, but the theory does not argue that a social revolution caused the withdrawal.[153] Rather, proponents of this framework theorize that indigenous Canaanites *gradually* left the urban centers, forming new Highland Settlements, and eventually becoming known as a new ethnic group, the Israelites. A key characteristic of this model is that indigenous Canaanite, or "urban refugees," migrated to the highlands and other groups did as well, including sedentarized nomads, *habiru*, the *shashu* (from around Egypt), and diverse immigrants from wider regions.[154] The process of settling the highlands and the subsequent new societal and ethnic formation would likely have taken considerable amounts of time.[155]

---

[153]McNutt, "Reconstructing the Society of Ancient Israel," 57.

[154]McNutt, "Reconstructing the Society of Ancient Israel," 57.

[155]Niels Peter Lemche argues that the Highland Settlements were a long-term development that spanned the whole Late Bronze Age. See Niels Peter

Though there are varied approaches and names given to the indigenous origins theory, the basic framework is now widely accepted among archaeologists and biblical scholars.[156] Robert Coote and Keith Whitelam propose a revision to the theory, arguing for a gradual development of the highland villages as a result of declining urban centers—not as a cause for their decline.[157] As the urban centers waned, generations of settlers left over time in order to produce their own food.[158] However, not all scholars wish to abandon the idea of an intentional withdrawal, even if they do not agree that it was a deliberate revolt.

Based on new archaeological evidence, Dever contends that the theory of an intentional withdrawal should be reconsidered because of the unstable situation at the end of the Bronze Age, which resulted in societal collapse that would have meant that villagers, farmers, *habiru*, and other impoverished and socially marginalized people would have had "little to lose" by withdrawing to the highlands.[159] For Dever, groups of Canaanite dissidents and opportunists went to the highland frontier to start a new way of life. Frontier areas are often developed in

Lemche, *Early Israel: Anthropological and Historical Studies on the Israelite Society before the Monarchy* (Leiden: E. J. Brill, 1985), 411–35.

[156]According to Dever, the *indigenous origins* theory "is sometimes called a 'dissolution' model . . . a 'sedentarized nomads' model (Finkelstein, Rainey, and others), or a 'mixed multitude' model (Killebrew and Dever)." Dever, *Beyond the Texts*, 222.

[157]Robert B. Coote and Keith W. Whitelam, *The Emergence of Early Israel in Historical Perspective* (Sheffield: Sheffield Phoenix, 2010).

[158]McNutt, *Reconstructing the Society of Ancient Israel*, 59.

[159]Dever pairs the idea of withdrawal with Gerhard and Jean Lenski's sociological theory of frontier spaces, suggesting that frontiers provide a "unique opportunity for departures from the sociocultural patterns so deeply entrenched in agrarian societies." He also argues that "*There may have existed an ideology that made revolution seem possible, even inevitable.*" Dever, *Beyond the Texts*, 225–26. Emphasis mine.

new ways, with new social and technological innovations, as evident in the Highland Settlements.[160] Even with nuanced modifications, the basic tenet of the indigenous origins framework remains: the majority of proto-Israelite people were most likely indigenous Canaanites seeking a better way of life on the heels of the collapse of Late Bronze Age civilizations. Their new beginning marked the start of what would later become the Israelite people and their religious traditions.

The interpretive frameworks discussed in this section illustrate both the variety and the complexity of ways that biblical scholars and archaeologists have attempted to synthesize archaeological evidence and biblical texts. While older frameworks, like the conquest theory, sought to support the historical accuracy of the biblical texts, newer frameworks, like the indigenous origins theory, suggest that the actual origins of the Hebrew people were quite different from biblical stories of the conquest of Canaan by Israelite outsiders (Josh 3–9).

Conclusion

The archaeological evidence indicates that new settlements emerged at the end of the Late Bronze Age and the beginning of the Iron Age in the highland regions of ancient Canaan. Many scholars' interpretations of the material evidence sug-

---

[160]As Dever explains, "New ways of life commonly develop in frontier areas, innovations are readily accepted, and older rigidities give way." He draws this quote from the 1978 work of Gerhard Lenski and Jean Lenski, *Human Societies: An Introduction to Macrosociology* (New York: McGraw-Hill, 1978). In it they observe that frontiers provide a "unique opportunity for departures from the sociocultural patterns so deeply entrenched in agrarian societies." Dever, *Beyond the Texts*, 226.

gest that the people living in these settlements were, in large part, indigenous Canaanites. Some biblical scholars have argued that the people inhabiting these settlements were proto-Israelite—that these peoples were made up of diverse groups of marginalized peoples who fled the Late Bronze Age Canaanite civilization that was ruled by the Egyptian Empire because of extreme socioeconomic oppression and chaotic societal disruptions caused by a dramatic climate change. This new start on the highland frontier gave settlers a chance to form a new society in contrast to the socially stratified conditions of empire.

The archaeological evidence is sparse, but it can tell us a little about the people who lived in certain locations and whether certain sites were inhabited during certain time periods. Biblical scholars have provided competing interpretations of the archaeological material over the last several decades. When seeking to undo conquest in Christian churches today, the indigenous origins theory provides a compelling interpretation of archaeological and biblical data that accounts for prior frameworks and provides a more nuanced and tempered lens for contemporary work. The indigenous origins interpretive framework will likely continue to develop, not least because so much is at stake in terms of contemporary faith communities that take the origins of the Hebrew people and the biblical texts seriously. I bring the indigenous origins theory forward as an interpretive lens for faith communities to interpret the interplay of archaeological evidence, the origins of the proto-Israelite people, and the continued influence of the Bible in much of the Western world.

From the indigenous origins framework, the Highland Settlements can be understood in the spirit of what Victor Turner calls a communitas movement, a social reform movement that aims to create better living and social conditions than current structures permit.[161] As such, the Highland Settlement material can be interpreted as a liberative origins narrative—the type that feminists argue is needed to help generate imagination for a more liberative present. Churches often examine their current praxis, seeking transformation in moments of change and decline. Such processes of change typically involve examining the past as a means to reconstitute the present. The Highland Settlements evidence provides a countermemory into the ancient past that can help prompt radical imagination and social change.

---

[161]Victor Turner, Roger D. Abrahams, and Alfred Harris, *The Ritual Process: Structure and Anti-Structure* (London: Taylor and Francis, 2017), 119–54.

3

Conquest in Context

If the origins of the Hebrew people in Canaan were a result of an indigenous and nonmilitaristic settlement process, why does the Bible depict Israelite origins as outsiders, as people who conquered Canaan through a Yahweh-ordained genocidal conquest? How did the biblical writers of the book of Joshua get their history so wrong? Can this historical discrepancy simply be attributed to a lapse in memory—a massive forgetting? Was something else at work?[1]

Decades of biblical scholarship have explored the differences in these two histories, and much research has been dedicated to understanding the historical context and likely

---

[1]Regina Schwartz asks similar questions, "How was the real (historical) story—whatever it was—so completely misremembered in the biblical narrative? Why was it covered up? Why weren't the ways in which Canaanites were really Israelites made more explicit, or the success of the revolutionaries recorded, instead of the stories that have been handed down to us of the bloody conquest of one people by another? And if the process was so peaceful, how did the story of violent invasion come to be? Whom did it serve, when and why?" Regina M. Schwartz, *The Curse of Cain: The Violent Legacy of Monotheism* (Chicago: University of Chicago Press, 1997), 155.

authorship of the Joshua narrative.[2] Such historical-critical scholarship on the book of Joshua provides insights into why the conquest narrative deviates so much from the historical settlement pattern attested to in the archaeological evidence.[3] While there is a broad amount of research on this subject, and not all agree on the details, there is some basic consensus on the fundamental contours of when and why the book of Joshua and the conquest narrative were written.

Historical-critical biblical scholarship provides insight into why certain biblical stories depict Israelite origins in a violent, militaristic way, whereas the archaeological evidence reveals a very different set of circumstances. Instead of misremembering, the historical discrepancy occurred through an intentional

---

[2]For a recent text that details this scholarship, see Thomas Römer, *The So-Called Deuteronomistic History: A Sociological, Historical, and Literary Introduction* (London: T&T Clark, 2005)—or for a more detailed review, see Erik Eynikel's *The Reform of King Josiah and the Composition of the Deuteronomistic History* (Leiden: E. J. Brill, 1996).

[3]William Dever explains, "The foregoing survey of the archaeological data leaves one, I think, with little choice. We must confront the fact that the external material evidence supports almost *nothing* of the biblical account of a large-scale, concerted Israelite military invasion of Canaan, either that of Numbers east of the Jordan, or of Joshua west of the Jordan. Of the more than forty sites that the biblical texts claim were conquered, no more than two or three of those that have been archaeologically investigated are even potential candidates for such an Israelite destruction in the entire period of *ca.* 1250–1150 B.C. . . . Yet even among people who are open-minded and willing to try to accommodate the archaeological data, legitimate questions remain. If the biblical stories as they stand do not give us adequate account of what *really* happened, how shall we reconstruct the early Israelite settlement? And if the stories are not 'true' in a factual sense, how did they come to be told, written, and preserved for so long in the first place? What did the writer editors of the Hebrew Bible think they were *doing*? And how have Jews and Christians been fooled for so long? . . . The theological issues simply cannot be sidestepped, as most archaeologists tend to think." William G. Dever, *Who Were the Early Israelites and Where Did They Come From?* (Grand Rapids: Eerdmans, 2003), 71–72.

reimagining of history to support the needs of a Judean monarchy over five hundred years after the establishment of the first Highland Settlement in the hills of Canaan. Moreover, it is likely that many people during this time *did* remember the settlement history of early Israel, but their voices were slowly drowned out as new historical stories were told, supported by people in power during a time of political turmoil during the Babylonian exile.

The Deuteronomistic History

The historical and political context that gave birth to the conquest story is a fascinating era with political calculations that rival those found in a *Game of Thrones* episode. This chapter explores the book of Joshua as part of a strategic, historiographic corpus of texts developed in the seventh century BCE in Judah, known as the Deuteronomistic History (DH). During this time, the Assyrian Empire, which had long dominated the region, began to crumble. In Assyria's wake, an elite group of Judeans, during the reign of King Josiah, saw an opportunity to reunite the two kingdoms of Israel and Judah into one expanded state, with Jerusalem as the capital. After years of Assyrian oppression and violence, the Judean political class began to dream of independence and expansion.[4] This is an understandable dream, given that the Assyrian Empire exercised a reign of terror for centuries.

The DH is a sweeping historical collection of texts, and the first edition was likely written during this intermittent

---

[4]David Carr uses the lens of trauma to understand the motives and actions of the seventh-century Judean leaders in his book *Holy Resilience: The Bible's Traumatic Origins* (New Haven, CT: Yale University Press, 2014). See chapter 3, "Judah's Survival," 41–66.

period as the Assyrian Empire weakened. It presents Josiah as the ideal king, even more ideal than well-known rulers like David and Solomon. The plot of the Deuteronomistic History crescendos at the Yahwistic cultic reforms of Josiah (detailed in 2 Kings 23), which were instituted in order to generate the resources needed to support a unified two-state expansion, not for the pious reasons that the Bible reports. The DH can be considered a practical theology of sorts—designed to help support the Judean nationalist and expansionist ambitions.[5] Just as some contemporary practical theologians develop new theologies, rituals, and practices to generate certain practical outcomes, so too, the authors of the conquest narrative developed a strategic historiographic and theological perspective aimed to shape imagination and practices in Judah during the seventh century BCE.[6]

Understanding the Judean context of the book of Joshua

---

[5]Contemporary practical theologians would not condone the development of violent texts to produce practical outcomes; however, I draw the parallel with practical theology because it helps to explain how these texts functioned in their context and helps to sever the idea that these texts are "factually" historical. Grace Jantzen explains the ideological function of the conquest narrative: "The stories of warfare and the extermination of others in the name of Yahweh who had chosen Israel as the special people of his covenant are therefore not to be read as real events. Rather, they are intended to help consolidate national identity by giving the people an imagined idealized past which enabled the weak and emergent nation to reconceive itself as the special people of God, in spite of her much more powerful neighbors and enemies (Perdue 1994)." Grace M. Jantzen, *Violence to Eternity*, ed. Jeremy Carrette and Morny Joy (London: Routledge, 2009), 115.

[6]David Carr argues that Josiah reworked the northern vision of Hosea and implemented his ideas in the Judah cult: "Josiah turns the ancient northern law book found in the temple into a theological version of the Assyrian covenant and leads the people to 'cut' that covenant with Yahweh. Where Hosea was an Israelite prophet who influenced Judeans, Josiah was a Judean king who enacted Hosea-like ideas, using a document originally from the north." Carr, *Holy Resilience*, 60.

affirms yet again that history matters. The importance of history is not a new insight developed by critical theorists in the last century. The seventh-century Judean political class knew this as well, which is why they used their resources to develop a new history of Israel's origins in Canaan to shape their culture in ways that supported their political ambitions. The conquest narrative was not written to accurately portray ancient Israelite history, but rather, in contemporary terms, it can be considered "fake news"—an ideological historiographic text that retroactively projected the political ambitions of elite seventh-century Judeans upon the screen of Israel's past.[7]

Though the book of Joshua purports to tell ancient Israelite history, it is far removed from the early Iron Age from which Israel emerged. For perspective, the DH was written roughly five hundred years after the formation of the early Hebrew Highland Settlements. Joshua himself is a character designed as a historical muse meant to be an ancient reflection of Josiah, who mirrors the Josianic political ambitions and cultic reforms.[8] As such, the book of Joshua is about coercion and control, attempting to "harness the energies of the population by invoking their loyalties through a sense of identity."[9] The

---

[7]For discussions on the narrative form of Joshua, see L. Daniel Hawk, "The Truth about Conquest: Joshua as History, Narrative, and Scripture," *Interpretation: A Journal of Bible and Theology* 66, no. 2 (April 2012): 129–40; Ian Douglas Wilson, "Conquest and Form: Narrativity in Joshua 5–11 and Historical Discourse in Ancient Judah," *Harvard Theological Review* 106, no. 3 (July 2013): 309–29.

[8]See Richard D. Nelson, "Josiah in the Book of Joshua," *Journal of Biblical Literature* 100, no. 4 (December 1981): 531–40; Marvin Sweeney, *King Josiah of Judah: The Lost Messiah of Israel* (Oxford: Oxford University Press, 2001).

[9]Lori Rowlett explains that the book of Joshua clearly depicts the Canaanites as "outsiders," as opposed to Israelite "insiders." The message is less about ethnicity and more that anyone can become an outsider—that is, "insiders who pose a threat to the hierarchy being asserted. The message is that the punishment of Otherness is death and that insiders can easily become outsiders

book clearly demarks insiders from outsiders, or "us" versus "them," with a rhetoric of violence that acts coercively to keep people within particular boundaries.[10] The book even closely mimics the style of Assyrian royal campaign inscriptions and Assyrian war rhetoric.[11]

(Others) by failure to submit." Rowlett also goes on to explain that the book also attempts to "win the voluntary loyalty of the people by making them feel a part of the collective entity." Lori Rowlett, *Joshua and the Rhetoric of Violence* (Sheffield, UK: Sheffield Academic Press, 1996), 12–13.

[10]Rowlett uses Michel Foucault's understanding of power relations and its application in "New Historicist" interpretation of texts as a means to understand the role and function of the book of Joshua in its seventh-century BCE context. As she explains, "A work of art will not only reflect the negotiations and exchanges of power taking place in the society which produced it but will also be a part of the process. Therefore, the text itself has an ideological function as an assertion of power which in turn affects the political environment of that context. The threat inherent in the Joshua text functions as an instrument of coercion, or at least encouragement, to submission." Rowlett, *Joshua and the Rhetoric of Violence*, 12.

[11]John Van Seters shows the parallels between Assyrian royal campaign inscriptions and the Joshua conquest narrative. He argues that the writers of Joshua would have been familiar with the Assyrian genre and leveraged it in their own historiographic work. John Van Seters, "Joshua's Campaign of Canaan and Near Eastern Historiography," *Scandinavian Journal of the Old Testament* 4, no. 2 (January 1, 1990): 1–12. David Carr states that Deuteronomy is "an ancient, post-Mosaic northern law book that was then modified by Josiah's scribes into an Assyrian-styled covenant between the people and their god Yahweh." Carr, *Holy Resilience*, 59–60. Many others also pick up on the similarity between Assyrian imperial inscriptions and the book of Joshua. See Rowlett, *Joshua and the Rhetoric of Violence*, 13; Richard Jude Thompson, *Terror of the Radiance: Aššur Covenant to YHWH Covenant*, CBO 258 (Fribourg: Academic Press, 2013); Ian Douglas Wilson, "Conquest and Form: Narrativity in Joshua 5–11 and Historical Discourse in Ancient Judah," *Harvard Theological Review* 106, no. 3 (July 2013): 312–13; K. Lawson Younger Jr., *Ancient Conquest Accounts: A Study in Ancient Biblical History Writing*, JSOTSup 98 (Sheffield: Sheffield Academic, 1990), 61–124.

The Structure and Content of Joshua

Joshua is part of the collection of books in the Bible known as the former prophets (Joshua, Samuel, Kings), which follows the Pentateuch (Genesis, Exodus, Leviticus, Numbers, Deuteronomy). The first six books of the Bible, sometimes known as the Hexateuch (the Pentateuch plus Joshua), string together an overarching historical narrative of the emergence of the Hebrew people in Canaan, beginning in primordial times; into the Abrahamic stories, the exodus from Egypt, and the Israelite wanderings in the wilderness; and concluding with the dramatic story of the Israelite conquest of Canaan. The book of Joshua as we have it now is likely the result of a lengthy process of additions and redactions since its original composition.[12] Overall, Joshua has a close connection with Deuteronomy through three key themes: Yahweh is the giver of the land; a theology of retribution that demands obedience to Yahweh (obedience leads to success and disobedience to failure); and the destruction and outright extermination of the existing peoples in the land.[13] Joshua has four distinct parts: a preamble or introduction to the conquest in a series of speeches (1:1–18), a depiction of military victories over the peoples of Canaan (2:1–12:24), land allotments given to each tribe (13:1–21:42), and a series of endings and a farewell speech that exhorts the Israelites to stay faithful to Yahweh (21:43–24).[14]

While Joshua speaks in a totalizing language about Israel's

---

[12]Hawk, *Joshua in 3D*, xx.
[13]Hawk, *Joshua in 3D*, xxi.
[14]Hawk, *Joshua in 3D*, xx–xxi.

conquest, there is also a quieter and somewhat subversive voice found within the book.[15] Commentators have widely noted that the story of Rahab does not follow the strict Deuteronomistic command to not intermingle with the Canaanite "others."[16] Here, in the very beginning of the story, Joshua's spies negotiate a deal with a Canaanite woman to save their lives and, in turn, to save hers (Josh 2). A marginalized Canaanite woman, Rahab, has come to the rescue of God's army and now they must rescue her; they will carry her with them so that she may continue to dwell among them (Josh 6:25). The Rahab story marks an ironic and "glaring internal contradiction between the warfare guidelines in Deut. 20:10–20 and this negotiated exception, which makes the Rahab story stick out like a sore thumb."[17] The story of Rahab is indicative of this other voice in the Joshua narrative, one that is not as confident in the Israelite story of conquest as other parts of the text are; Rahab, essentially, undermines the story from within.[18] This

---

[15]Hawk details the differences in these two opposing voices found in the text, what he calls a dominant voice and a subtle voice. The subtle or whispering voice "subverts the strident voice of militarism, legalism, and superiority by drawing our attention to instances of disobedience to the commands of Moses (as in making forbidden covenants with Rahab and the Gibeonites) and reporting unsuccessful efforts to subdue the indigenous peoples (15:63; 16:10; 17:12–13; 20:47) and possess their lands (13:1–7). Hawk, *Joshua in 3D*, xxii–xxiii.

[16]Carolyn Sharp explains, "The Canaanites are irrevocably ensconced in the midst of Israel from the very first military foray. How can this triumphant historical story be written when it has already been unwritten in the first chapter? . . . We have here the ironizing and unraveling of plot by the very characters figured in it." Carolyn J. Sharp, *Irony and Meaning in the Hebrew Bible* (Bloomington, IN: Indiana University Press, 2009), 102.

[17]Robert G. Boling, *Joshua* (Garden City, NY: Doubleday, 1982), 150.

[18]Daniel Hawk explains that the story of Rahab "has received a positive reading by virtually all commentators. The readings generally ignore or downplay the transgression that the oath represents and focus instead on the faith of Rahab or her acclamations of praise to Yahweh." Daniel Hawk, "Strange

alternate narrative voice that shows up in Joshua indicates that the book went through a series of edits and redactions before landing on the form that we have now.[19] However, despite the ironic and subversive voice present in the story, the overarching Deuteronomistic themes of land-taking, retribution, and conquest continue to dominate the final form of Joshua, and these are the key plot and theological elements that influenced an imperialistic Christian imagination.[20]

Historiography and Politics:
The Deuteronomistic History and Josianic Reforms

Understanding the historical-political context into which the conquest narrative was born, it is easier to recognize how the conquest narrative is a dangerous story—a text of terror—that has undergirded support for genocide and imperial domination far away from and long after Judah in the seventh

---

House Guests: Rahab, Lot, and the Dynamics of Deliverance," in *Reading between the Texts: Intertextuality and the Hebrew Bible,* ed. Danna Nolan Fewell (Louisville, KY: Westminster/John Knox, 1992), 97n8.

[19]Sharp explains the ideological contradiction the story of Rahab introduces into the narrative: "The political rhetoric of the holy-war ideology requires that the Israelites take no prisoners. Yet interactions with outsiders are required from the very first moment in order to assess the risks—so negotiation, with its attendant dangers of cooperation and capitulation, is necessary" (Sharp, *Irony and Meaning,* 101–2).

[20]Robert B. Coote pointedly states that "much of the Book of Joshua is repulsive, starting with ethnic cleansing, the savage dispossession and genocide of native peoples and the massacre of women and children—all not simply condoned but ordered by God. These features are worse than abhorrent; they are far beyond the pale. Excoriable deeds and many others of at least questionable justifiability have been committed with the sanction of the book of Joshua such as the decimation of the Native American peoples." Robert B. Coote, "The Book of Joshua," in *The New Interpreters Bible*, vol. 2 (Nashville: Abingdon, 1994), 578.

century BCE.[21] What were the factors that led to an edition of the Deuteronomistic History that included the book of Joshua and the cultic reforms during the reign of King Josiah? This section provides a description of the context, events, and texts discussed above that situate the book of Joshua as an artifact from seventh century BCE in Judah.

After Assyria conquered the northern kingdom of Israel in 722 BCE, the southern kingdom of Judah and its capital city, Jerusalem, experienced an influx both of people and economic resources, as northern refugees migrated to Judah.[22] During the century of Assyrian control of Israel in the north, Judah's relationship with Assyria vacillated between defiance and cooperative engagement.[23] During this period, Judah became an economic hub tied into the Assyrian economy by mass-producing olive oil and distributing luxury goods from Arabia.[24] The economic influx created a new social strata of

---

[21]I borrow the phrase "text of terror" from Phyllis Trible, who published a groundbreaking feminist biblical study that explores violent texts in the Hebrew Bible: *Texts of Terror: Literary-Feminist Readings of Biblical Narratives*, Overtures to Biblical Theology 13 (Philadelphia: Fortress, 1984).

[22]Finkelstein and Silberman explain: "The city of Jerusalem specifically experienced an extreme population expansion and began to morph into much different place than it had previously been: "Jerusalem was transformed from a modest highland town of about ten or twelve acres to a huge urban area of 150 acres of closely packed houses, workshops, and public buildings. In demographic terms, the city's population may have increased as much as fifteen times, form about one thousand to fifteen thousand inhabitants." Israel Finkelstein and Neil Asher Silberman, *The Bible Unearthed: Archaeology's New Vision of Ancient Israel and the Origin of its Sacred Texts* (New York: Simon and Schuster, 2002), 243.

[23]For a good overview of the economic and political situation in seventh-century BCE Judah, see Israel Finkelstein and Neil Asher Silberman, *The Bible Unearthed: Archaeology's New Vision of Ancient Israel and the Origin of Its Sacred Texts* (New York: Simon and Schuster, 2002), 251–74.

[24]According to Finkelstein and Silberman, "The question is, where did this wealth and apparent movement toward full state formation come from?

Judean economic elites for the first time.[25] Prior to Assyrian influence, Judah and Israel lacked elite economic resources. As already noted, the Assyrian Empire had long dominated the region yet was in the process of decline during this time.[26] In turn, Egypt again began to gain control in the region, largely leaving Judah alone because of its location in the highland regions. The Egyptians were mostly interested in the fertile lowlands along the Mediterranean shore.[27] In this destabilized political environment, other states took the opportunity to gain power and dominance in the region. During this period, newly burgeoning economic elites and leaders of Judah aspired "to certain political autonomy, or at least to encourage national-istic dreams among certain circles."[28] Here, the Judean rulers

---

The inescapable conclusion is that Judah suddenly cooperated with and even integrated itself into the economy of the Assyrian empire. . . . There is good reason to believe that new markets were opened to Judahite goods, stimulat-ing intensified production of oil and wine. As a result, Judah went through an economic revolution, from a traditional system based on the village and clan to cash-cropping and industrialization under state centralization. Wealth began accumulating in Judah, especially in Jerusalem, where the kingdom's diplomatic and economic policies were determined and where the institu-tions of the nation were controlled" (Finkelstein and Silberman, *The Bible Unearthed*, 245). See also page 267 for further discussion.

[25]Finkelstein and Silberman note that evidence of new, elaborate burial practices mostly in Jerusalem during this time period indicates a sudden ac-cumulation of wealth, a discrepancy in social status, and the emergence of a national elite. *The Bible Unearthed*, 245–46.

[26]Finkelstein and Silberman explain that the factors leading to Assyrian decline are not agreed upon by scholars, but nevertheless, "Assyrian power clearly began to decline near the end of the reign of the last great Assyrian king, Ashurbanipal (669–627 BCE), due to the pressure of mounted nomadic Scythian tribes on the northern borders of the empire and continuous conflicts with the subject peoples of Babylonia and Elam on the East" (Finkelstein and Silberman, *The Bible Unearthed*, 282). See also Rowlett, *Joshua and Rhetoric of Violence*, 11.

[27]Finkelstein and Silberman, *The Bible Unearthed*, 283.

[28]Römer, *The So-Called Deuteronomistic History*, 70–71.

envisioned a unified kingdom and dreamed of consolidating Judah in the south with Israel's lost territories in the north.[29]

As David Carr explains, long-sustained trauma likely played a part in Judah's dreams for a unified state. After witnessing the Assyrians terrorize and destroy the northern kingdom of Israel in 722 BCE, Judah became a vassal state to Assyria for several decades and had to pay a steep tribute. Judah responded to decades of oppression by seeking to create a secure state in Assyria's decline.[30] Carr argues that the Deuteronomists were influenced by the text of the northern prophet Hosea, who blamed Israel's destruction by Assyria on the worship of other gods. Judah appropriated Hosea's Assyrian-influenced ideology and applied it to their own Judean context: perhaps if Judah could obey Yahweh, then they would be rewarded with regaining Israel in the north and be secured from attack and destruction. They were seeking control in an out-of-control environment. "Hosea," Carr notes, "had called for an Assyrian-like love of Yahweh alone; Josiah enforced it."[31] Judah's response is understandable after centuries of generational trauma inflicted by one of the most violent and terrorizing empires of their time. Yet, because of the way Western history unfolded, the Deuteronomistic texts, born from this communal trauma, lived far beyond their seventh-century Judean context in unimaginable ways. The

---

[29]Mario Liverani, *Israel's History and the History of Israel* (London: Routledge, 2014), xvi–xvii.

[30]David M. Carr writes about the traumatic origins of the Deuteronomistic monotheistic theology as a product of Assyrian domination and response to this trauma. See in particular his discussions in chapters 2 and 3 of *Holy Resilience*, 24–66. In particular, Carr states that "imperial trauma thus powered and shaped religious trauma. Judeans had been terrorized over the years into renouncing alliances with foreigners. Now the same cultural form used to enforce that renunciation, the imperial covenant, was used by Josiah to require renunciation of gods and ancient sanctuaries" (60).

[31]Carr, *Holy Resilience*, 60.

Deuteronomistic ideology, directly influenced by the Assyrian Empire through Hosea, has had incredible impact throughout the last twenty-five hundred years, as their texts became part of the sacred book of Christendom.

King Josiah and the Deuteronomistic History

Second Kings 22:23 reports that King Amon of Judah was murdered by the servants in his house. In retaliation, the so-called people of the land seek justice for Amon and installed his eight-year-old son, Josiah, to the throne. These mysterious "people of the land" are thought to be the Deuteronomists, the group responsible for fashioning the Deuteronomistic History. Theories abound about the Deuteronomists' identity. Where they a school? An elite class of Judeans disguised as the people of the land? Neo-Assyrian scribes? More than likely, they were made up of some combination of priests, scribes, and important elite families in Jerusalem.[32] Placing an eight-year-old Josiah on the throne ensured that these elite groups were really in control of Judah at the time. Additionally, they were likely the group that launched the coup against Amon even though the Bible reports it differently.[33]

King Josiah is an important biblical character, but he

---

[32]Thomas Römer speculates about who was in control of Judah at this time: "If there is any truth to the biblical report according to which Josiah came to the throne at age eight (2 Kgs 22.1), this probably means that the real power was in the priests, scribes and some important families at the royal center. The Deuteronomistic school probably participated in this coalition of members from these different social groups, with a clear nationalistic and Zionist orientation" (*The So-Called Deuteronomistic History*), 70–71. See also Israel Finkelstein and Neil Asher Silberman, "A Great Reformation 639–586 BCE," in *The Bible Unearthed*, 275–295, for one discussion on this topic. Or Richard Jude Thompson, *Terror of the Radiance: Aššur Covenant to YHWH Covenant* (Fribourg: Academic Press, 2013), where he proposes that the DH may have been written as neo-Assyrian propaganda.

[33]Carr, *Holy Resilience*, 52.

lacks the popularity and name recognition of more commonly known biblical kings like David and Solomon and other biblical characters such as Moses, Abraham, Jacob, and even Joshua. Despite his lack of popular notoriety, the story of Josiah and his reign (639–609 BCE), as well as the cultic reforms he supposedly enacted during his reign, are pivotal for Hebrew Bible studies.[34]

During the decline of the Assyrian Empire, Josiah, the Deuteronomists, or both saw an opportunity to bid for power in the region. However, in order to have sufficient financial and militaristic resources to make such a bid, they needed to reorganize Judah more like a centralized imperial state.[35] By centralizing the practice of the Yahwistic religion around the capital city, Jerusalem, through a series of cultic reforms, the Deuteronomists were able to regionally centralize Judah.[36] The Deuteronomistic History details the cultic reforms, providing a window into this era.

Second Kings 22:8–23:27 reports that Josiah established a temple renovation project during the eighteenth year of his reign. During these renovations, it is reported that a "lost" book of the law was found and taken to the king. Upon hearing the book read aloud, Josiah was aggrieved as he heard that the cult of Yahwism had strayed from its traditional practices. He tore his clothes and had the priests seek out the prophetess Huldah to inquire about the book. She confirms that indeed the Israelites had abandoned traditional cultic practices. Through

---

[34]Sweeney, *King Josiah of Judah*, 3.

[35]Shigeyuki Nakanose, *Josiah's Passover: Sociology and the Liberating Bible* (Maryknoll, NY: Orbis, 1993), 50; Wes Howard-Brook, *"Come Out, My People!": God's Call out of Empire in the Bible and Beyond* (Maryknoll, NY: Orbis, 2010), 183.

[36]Römer, *The So-Called Deuteronomistic History*, 54–55; Rowlett, *Joshua and the Rhetoric of Violence*, 183.

Huldah, Yahweh declares, "Because they have abandoned me and have made offerings to other gods, so that they have provoked me to anger with all the work of their hands, therefore my wrath will be kindled against this place, and it will not be quenched" (2 Kings 22:17).

In response to Huldah's prophecy, Josiah then institutes a series of cultic reforms to return the cult to its "correct" traditional practices. Second Kings 23 describes a harrowing list of violent reforms, what biblical scholars commonly refer to as the Deuteronomistic or Josianic reforms. First, Josiah reformed the Jerusalem Temple by removing any remnants of worship of Asherah, the goddess consort to Yahweh (2 Kings 23:4–6).[37] Then Josiah enacted reforms in the wider region, destroying all other cultic sites, like the one at Bethel (2 Kings 23:13–15). According to the text, Josiah did not stop at just the destruction of cultic sites. The narrative also reports that his reforms involved the killing of the priests at these cultic sites:

> Moreover, Josiah removed all the shrines of the high places that were in the towns of Samaria, which kings of Israel had made, provoking the LORD to anger; he did to them just as he had done at Bethel. He slaughtered on the altars all the priests of the high places who were there, and burned human bones on them. Then he returned to Jerusalem. (2 Kings 23:19–20)

Josiah's reforms involved both destruction and the construction of new rituals aimed at Judah's centralization, like the practice of Passover that had supposedly been abandoned

---

[37]See the following texts for the substantial evidence that supports this: Saul M. Olyan, *Asherah and the Cult of Yahweh in Israel* (Atlanta: Scholars Press, 1988); William G. Dever, *Did God Have a Wife? Archaeology and Folk Religion in Ancient Israel* (Grand Rapids: Eerdmans, 2005).

since ancient times. According to 2 Kings 23, the Passover had been described in the Book of the Covenant but had not been practiced since the time of the judges:

> The king commanded all the people, "Keep the passover to the LORD your God as prescribed in this book of the covenant." No such passover had been kept since the days of the judges who judged Israel, even during all the days of the kings of Israel and of the kings of Judah; but in the eighteenth year of King Josiah this passover was kept to the LORD in Jerusalem. (2 Kings 23:21–23)

The Josianic reforms involved burning cultic elements, razing cultic sites, and slaughtering priests—a truly brutal reformation. During the reforms, Josiah also instituted the Passover pilgrimage to Jerusalem as a central Yahwistic practice, which brought the rural populations to Jerusalem.

Although the Bible tells the story of finding a lost book during a temple renovation and then a series of cultic reforms that follow, the historical accuracy of both is questionable. First, the book-find motif is likely a fabrication as it follows a common pattern found in other ancient Near Eastern literature employed to legitimate religious, economic, or political changes. It was not uncommon for supposedly "old books" to be found by kings undertaking restoration projects.[38] The book-find motif gave newly written texts historical authority by falsely positioning them as ancient. The 2 Kings account clearly mimics this approach.[39] The motif made the contempo-

---

[38] Römer, *The So-Called Deuteronomistic History,* 51–52. See also Howard-Brook, *"Come Out, My People!,"* 183; Liverani, *Israel's History,* 175.

[39] Römer explains that similar motifs can be found in Egyptian and Babylonian literature. See *The So-Called Deuteronomistic History,* 51–53, for more details concerning other ancient sources that utilize this "book-finding" motif.

rary words of the Deuteronomists appear "ancient," providing legitimacy to these newly edited or written texts. The book identified in 2 Kings was likely some form of what is now the book of Deuteronomy because it supports the ideology of centralization, depicted as the Law of Moses, which is the implicit driver of the Josianic reforms.[40]

Second, the book-find and the resulting reforms were not undertaken with the sole motivation of purifying the cult. The text production and reforms of Josiah and the Deuteronomists

---

[40]Howard-Brook notes that "scholars are virtually unanimous in understanding the specific book found to be a form of Deuteronomy" (*"Come Out, My People!,"* 183). David Carr contends that an earlier version of Deuteronomy probably came from the north since it has initially that Gerizim is the official site of worship, which is located in Israel. However, this early form of Deuteronomy was expanded and reworked by the Josianic scribes, making it the center of the Josianic covenant and reforms (*Holy Resilience*, 59). Marvin Sweeney explains that "the book of Deuteronomy represents Josiah's attempt to revise the system of Israelite law in order to enhance the religious, economic, and political power of the centralized state and thereby to unite the people around the Jerusalem temple and the house of David" (*King Josiah of Judah*, 19). Thomas Römer also explains that "Early Jewish commentators, as well as some Church Fathers, already identified the book mentioned in 2 Kings 22–23 as the book of Deuteronomy, since the acts of Josiah and the ideology of centralization, which sustains his 'reform,' seem to agree with the prescriptions of the Deuteronomic Law (cf. e.g., Deut. 17.1–3 and 2 Kgs. 23.4–5; Deut. 12.2–3 and 2 Kgs. 23.6, 14; Deut. 23.18 and 2 Kgs. 23.7; Deut. 18.10–11 and 2 Kgs. 23.24). This identification was then used in the nineteenth and twentieth centuries as a way of locating the primitive edition of Deuteronomy at the time of Josiah, in the last third of the seventh century. According to the *pia fraus* ('pious lie') theory, as advocated by Wellhausen and others, the first edition of Deuteronomy was written in order to promote the Josianic reform, disguised as Moses' testament and hidden in the temple so as to be quickly discovered" (*The So-Called Deuteronomistic History,* 50). See also Joseph Blenkinsopp, *Sage, Priest, Prophet: Religious and Intellectual Leadership in Ancient Israel* (Louisville, KY: Westminster John Knox, 1995), 159; Liverani, *Israel's History*, 175; Richard D. Nelson, *The Double Redaction of the Deuteronomistic History*, JSOTSup 18 (Sheffield: JSOT Press, Department of Biblical Studies, University of Sheffield, 1981), 121; Rowlett, *Joshua and the Rhetoric of Violence*, 15.

is considered to be an elaborate form of propaganda developed to support their political expansionist ambitions through the centralization of the cult around the Jerusalem Temple.[41] The reformed cult was a means to centralize the religion. With a centralized religion, economic resources could be cultivated: "Josiah needed a 'religious' justification to mask this raw economic motivation."[42] From this perspective, the book of Deuteronomy can be understood as an ideological "attempt to revise the system of Israelite law in order to enhance the religious, economic, and political power of the centralized state and thereby to unite the people around the Jerusalem temple and the house of David."[43]

---

[41]Finkelstein and Silberman explain that the withdrawal from Assyria in the north created an opportunity for Judah to try and establish a Pan-Israelite state, but that "such an ambitious plan would require active and powerful propaganda. The book of Deuteronomy established the unity of the people of Israel and the centrality of their national cult place, but it was the Deuteronomistic History and parts of the Pentateuch that would create an epic saga to express the power and passion of a resurgent Judah's dreams" (*The Bible Unearthed*, 283). Lori Rowlett does not use the word "propaganda" but its meaning is implied when she describes the goal of the book of Joshua: "Although Joshua relates a story of the assertion of power through violent conquest, it does not function primarily as national battle epic nor as an anti-foreigner polemic, although these are elements of the story. Rather, those who produced the text used the rhetoric of warfare and nationalism as an encouragement and a threat, aimed at their own population, to submit voluntarily to the central authority of a government struggling to organize itself and create its own ideological framework of inclusion" (Rowlett, *Joshua and the Rhetoric of Violence*, 11). For further discussion, see also Frank Moore Cross, *Canaanite Myth and Hebrew Epic* (Cambridge, MA: Harvard University Press, 1973); Norbert Lohfink, "Kerygmata des Deuteronomistischen Geschichtswerks," in Lohfink, *Studien zum Deuteronomium und zur deuteronomistischen Literatur II*, SBA.AT 12 (Stuttgart: Katholisches Bibelwerk, 1991); Steven L. McKenzie, *The Trouble with Kings: The Composition of the Book of Kings in the Deuteronomistic History*, Supplements to Vetus Testamentum 42 (Leiden: E. J. Brill, 1991), 150; Römer, *So-Called Deuteronomistic History*, 42–43.

[42]Howard-Brook, *"Come Out, My People!,"* 183.

[43]Sweeney, *King Josiah of Judah*, 19.

The Passover, which was likely an old pastoral festival, was transformed by Deuteronomist ideology into a pilgrimage feast, which enforced people from the entire region to come and worship in Jerusalem; it also connected the newly instituted pilgrimage into an existing exodus from Egypt tradition.[44] Again, this institution of the Passover can be understood as a form of ideological practical theology. It functioned as a centralizing practice, which strengthened Judah's resources and the primacy of Jerusalem as the region's central political and religious city.[45] During the Passover, pilgrims could be forced to pay taxes in Jerusalem, which would fund a centralized administration and military.[46] While the extent of the Josianic reforms remains unclear, it does seem plausible that some sort of reform did occur during this time.[47]

---

[44]Schwartz explains that the conquest explicitly references the exodus tradition; however, rather than focusing on a flight to freedom, the book is about Joshua attaining power and authority: "The opening chapters of the Book of Joshua reawaken the memory of the exodus explicitly, casting it in that context of conquest. Instead of the Sea of Reeds, the waters of the river Jordan are now parted, and instead of the Israelites fleeing their oppressors on the ground, here the priests carry the ark of the covenant through the Jordan on dry ground. Throughout, the passage is self-consciously shaping a new memory that is intended to be rehearsed to future generations." Schwartz, *Curse of Cain*, 149–50. According to Liverani, "The transformation of Passover into a pilgrimage feast (*hag*) is probably an innovation by Josiah intended to enforce the gathering of worshipers from the whole land at the central sanctuary. The idea of connecting it to the founding event of the 'exodus from Egypt' is to be attributed to the Deuteronomist ideology." Liverani, *Israel's History and the History of Israel,* 177.

[45]Liverani, *Israel's History and the History of Israel,* 177.

[46]Howard-Brook, *"Come Out, My People!,"* 183; Nakanose, *Josiah's Passover,* 50.

[47]As Römer explains, "The biblical presentation of Josiah and his reign cannot be taken as a document of primary evidence. On the other hand, some indicators suggest nevertheless that some attempts to introduce cultic and political changes took place under Josiah." *The So-Called Deuteronomistic History,* 55.

In addition to revising an early form of Deuteronomy and enacting cultic reforms, it is also likely that some early version of the DH was produced by the Deuteronomists during the time.[48] While there is still much uncertainty on how many editions of the DH exist and when they were written and redacted, ultimately the details of editions and dating are not of key concern.[49] What is important is that an early edition of the DH was written in the seventh century, shaping Israelite history in such a way that Josiah is presented as the ideal king, even over and against David, and containing a version of the Joshua conquest narrative.[50] Interpreted through the lens of the seventh-century Deuteronomist and Josianic expansionist plans, Joshua reads as a document that lays out how a newly unified pan-Israelite state could be organized. Rather than reporting an ancient conquest, the book of Joshua communi-

---

[48]Marvin Sweeney notes that the author of the DH "shapes the entire work according to a well-conceived historiographical plan for the work as a whole. . . . This is of particular importance for establishing the existence of a Josianic edition of the work insofar as the preceding analysis notes that Joshua stands as a model for Josiah." Sweeney, *King Josiah of Judah,* 25. The following is a list of others who make an argument for a first edition of the Deuteronomistic History as being produced during the Josianic era: Frank Moore Cross, *Canaanite Myth and Hebrew Epic* (Cambridge, MA: Harvard University Press, 1973); McKenzie, *The Trouble with Kings,* 150; Nelson, "Josiah in the Book of Joshua"; Nelson, *The Double Redaction of the Deuteronomistic History,* Römer, *The So-Called Deuteronomistic History.*

[49]There are many theories that discuss how many editions of the DH existed, when and where they were written, and why. A cursory review of the scholarship in this arena reveals an alphabet soup of sources and theories, as scholar Ronald Harman Akenson notes, "Each has its tiny siglum, which, like the Masonic handshake, is known only to the initiates. Baruch Halpern comments ironically on the 'welter of sigla' and lists some of the more prominent of the new codes—Dtr, Dtr1, Dtr2, Dtr2, Dtr(hez), Dtr(jos), Dtr(x), DtrG, DtrH, DtrN, DtrP, E(Dtr)n, E(Dtr)p, E(Dtr)x, H, H(Dtr)het, H(Dtr)x, JE, M+, M–, Rdtr, Rdt3, SDeb. . . ." Akenson, *Surpassing Wonder,* 34.

[50]Nelson, "Josiah in the Book of Joshua"; Sweeney, *King Josiah of Judah*; Rowlett, *Joshua and the Rhetoric of Violence.*

cates the seventh-century Deuteronomistic ideology, with its key goals of administrative centralization, political expansion, and obeying Yahweh as a means to ensure its security and success. Understood as a key character in the larger DH corpus, Joshua can be understood as a historical proto-Josiah: he is a royal character who succeeds Moses, leads the Israelites into a holy war against the Canaanites, and enacts the Passover.[51] The Passover celebration of Josiah clearly mimics the one conducted by Joshua in Joshua 5:13–15.[52] Their connection is further linked by their names, which are similar in Hebrew.[53]

By creating a history of Israel to match seventh-century Deuteronomistic political goals, the DH, and specifically the book of Joshua, obfuscates the emergence of the Hebrew people in Canaan as a largely peaceful, indigenous Canaanite Highland Settlement pattern, who emerged as a response to political and ecological challenges found at the collapse of the Late Bronze Age. In a complete contrast, the DH depicts the Israelites not as indigenous Canaanites but as outsiders. Moreover, the Israelites are portrayed as a marauding, militaristic group, mimicking Assyrian imperialistic conquests of land and peoples.[54] As already discussed, Assyrian ideology

---

[51]Richard D. Nelson draws explicit parallels between Joshua and Josiah and argues that Joshua is a proto-Josiah. As Nelson explains, Joshua serves as a "forerunner to Josiah, providing an explicit historical precedence for Josiah's revolutionary reforming passover." Nelson, "Josiah in the Book of Joshua," 537. Others draw a similar conclusion. See: R. B. Coote and M. P. Coote, *Power, Politics and the Making of the Bible: An Introduction* (Minneapolis: Fortress, 1990), 63–64; Frank Moore Cross, *Canaanite Myth and Hebrew Epic* (Cambridge, MA: Harvard University Press, 1973); Rowlett, *Joshua and the Rhetoric of Violence*, 13, 181; Sweeney, *King Josiah of Judah*, 11.

[52]Rowlett, *Joshua and the Rhetoric of Violence*, 14.

[53]Howard-Brook notes the similarity in the Hebrew names Joshua and Josiah as indicative of Joshua as a prefiguring character to Josiah. Howard-Brook, *"Come Out, My People!,"* 183.

[54]For comparisons with Assyrian practices, see John Van Seters, "Joshua's

and practice, in part, influenced the Deuteronomistic texts, which were written centuries after the Highland Settlement period. Such a vision of history contradicts the archaeological record and is an anachronism: the imperial-conquest vision of the Deuteronomists, which they retroactively projected onto Hebrew origins, could not possibly be historically accurate to the early Iron Age. The Assyrian Empire first introduced violent conquest campaigns in the region during their imperial campaigns several centuries after the emergence of the Hebrew Highland Settlements in Canaan.[55] Such conquests were not plausible prior to the Assyrian Empire.

Herem

The following excerpt from Joshua describes the Israelite destruction of the city of Ai and is illustrative of the violent, genocidal imaginary found in Joshua that mimics Assyrian ideology:

> When Israel had finished slaughtering all the inhabitants of Ai in the open wilderness where they pursued them, and when all of them to the very last had fallen by the edge of the sword, all Israel returned to Ai, and attacked it with the edge of the sword. The total of those who fell that day, both men and women, was twelve thousand— all the people of Ai. For Joshua did not draw back his

---

Campaign of Canaan and Near Eastern Historiography," *Scandinavian Journal of the Old Testament* 4, no. 2 (January 1, 1990): 1–12. Also David Carr's perspective in *Holy Resilience* on the influence of Assyrian ideology on Hosea and subsequently Judah is instructive.

[55]Thompson argues that the covenant and conquest ideas in the DH could not have originated "from the humble origins of the hill country in Judah," but were rather influenced by the later Hittites and Assyrians. Thompson, *Terror of the Radiance,* 230.

hand, with which he stretched out the sword, until he had utterly destroyed all the inhabitants of Ai. Only the livestock and the spoil of that city Israel took as their booty, according to the word of the LORD that he had issued to Joshua. So Joshua burned Ai, and made it forever a heap of ruins, as it is to this day. And he hanged the king of Ai on a tree until evening; and at sunset Joshua commanded, and they took his body down from the tree, threw it down at the entrance of the gate of the city, and raised over it a great heap of stones, which stands there to this day. (Josh 8:24–29)

This is one example of many that describe the death and destruction that the Israelites inflicted upon the indigenous Canaanites. The death of the Canaanites is part of a divine sacrifice, called *herem* in Hebrew, which means that the Canaanites, their cities, and their possessions are all devoted to destruction (or killed) as an offering to Yahweh (see, e.g., Josh 6:15–21).[56] The concept of the *herem* as it was used in the Hebrew Bible and in surrounding Near Eastern contexts paradoxically gives value to enemies by offering them as a sacrifice to Yahweh, rather than assuming that their lives are worthless.[57] While the *herem* provides some intrinsic value to the lives of the Canaanites, by far it does not outweigh the violent "othering" and the divine justification of genocide perpetuated by the text.

---

[56]Susan Niditch, *War in the Hebrew Bible* (New York: Oxford University Press, 1995), 35–40. Here Susan Niditch explains in-depth the Hebrew concept of *herem* in its ancient Near Eastern context.

[57]Niditch, *War in the Hebrew Bible*, 50. Niditch explains that the suggestion that the *herem* paradoxically gives value to human life puts interpreters into the "uncomfortable position of appearing somehow sympathetic to the ban as sacrifice."

Exile

After all the creative efforts of producing the Deuteronomis-tic History and reforms during the Josianic reign, the Judean expansionist goals did not come to fruition. A united pan-Israelite state was never achieved. Indeed, in what seems to be his first military campaign, King Josiah meets the Egyptians in Megiddo and is killed on the battlefield by Pharaoh Neco (2 Kings 23:29–30).[58] Shortly thereafter, the power vacuum that occurred with the withdrawal of the Assyrians was filled by the Babylonians, who went on the offensive after the decline of the Assyrian Empire. Judah would soon become a vassal to Babylon (605 BCE), and eventually Jerusalem would be conquered and the Judean and Israelite elites expelled from Jerusalem during the Babylonian exile (c. 587–539 BCE).

The exiles in Babylon compiled the texts and histories of Israel and Judah to consolidate their textual traditions after they lost both their homeland and temple. Schwartz notes that "exile induced a crisis, and one result of that crisis was that authority became attached to a set of narratives rather than to a geopolitical configuration. Thereafter, the *narratives*, instead of the nation, became identity-defining."[59] The newly devel-oped Deuteronomistic texts became a central corpus of the texts gathered in one place during the exile, which meant that the Deuteronomist ideology became enshrined in the textual tradition as it was carried forward. The DH projected a violent history of origins upon the Israelite past that essentially paved over the Highland Settlement period. The settlements history was largely lost, and evidence of the settlement period found

---

[58]Liverani, *Israel's History*, 174.
[59]Schwartz, *Curse of Cain*, 145. Emphasis added.

only in glimpses of the exodus story, the stories of Judges, and the Hebrew prophetic traditions. Until the last century, the settlements story was not recovered, and only then it was recovered through the uncovering of their Iron Age I material assemblages. While the Deuteronomists ultimately did not achieve their imperialist goals, they did manage to implant their ideological and cultic changes within the Yahwistic tradition, as the Deuteronomistic History survived and became a core part of the Hebrew Bible.

The Deuteronomistic History
as a Historical Rebranding

The DH and Josianic reforms can be understood as political propaganda, a form of ideological practical theology, and, borrowing a term from graphic design, a historical *rebranding*. Through their written materials, the Deuteronomists told new historical stories that effectively rebranded their history. They were influenced by Assyrian ideology and reimagined their history in the image of Assyria. The Deuteronomistic book of Joshua reshaped the memory of a largely nonmilitaristic settlement pattern into a violent and militaristic one. Through the Deuteronomistic texts, "The exodus from bondage is remembered as a conquest of a new land."[60] Just as contemporary businesses go through rebranding processes to communicate their brand's story more effectively to audiences, the Deuteronomists deployed a new history to support their contemporary goals of creating a pan-Israelite state in the

---

[60]Schwartz, *Curse of Cain*, 149. Here Schwartz is influenced by the work of Michael Fishbane and his study of the Exodus narrative found in *Biblical Interpretation in Ancient Israel* (Oxford: Clarendon, 1985), 358–68.

wake of Assyrian withdrawal from the north.[61] They created a story to back their nation-building goals.

By rebranding their history, Deuteronomists also rebranded the Israelite cult and practices, developing a Yahweh-only tradition that was based in Jerusalem. The list of Josianic reforms in 2 Kings 23 provides a window into Israelite cultic practice before the reforms, which included multiple cultic sites and the worship of Yahweh's consort Asherah.[62] Evidence of goddess worship is prevalent in the archaeological record in Israel and Judah, as household figurines of Asherah are ubiquitous throughout the Iron Age.[63] By declaring the Israelite cult to

---

[61]Storytelling is a particularly powerful medium to convey messages that can move people into action. The Deuteronomistic History contains historical stories written in such a way to support political and religious reforms in the seventh century. Contemporary branding practices draw on the power of storytelling to motivate consumer practices. The book *Building a Storybrand* discusses the interconnection of story and branding. Donald Miller, *Building a Storybrand: Clarify Your Message So Customers Will Listen* (New York: HarperCollins Leadership, 2017).

[62]By writing down the details of their reform, the Deuteronomists left a textual archive of the very practices they were trying to eradicate—thus opening a window into the cultic practices of popular folk-tradition in late seventh-century BCE Judah. As William Dever explains, the writers of 2 Kings 23 catalog a long list of reform items and "in describing these 'pagan practices' they inadvertently give us valuable eyewitness details. . . . What we have in II Kings 23 is nothing less than an 'inventory' of the religious practices of *most* people in ancient Israel, not only toward the very end of the monarchy, but as they undoubtedly had been in place from the beginning (Asherah had been tolerated in the Temple until now)." Dever, *Did God Have a Wife?*, 212.

[63]James Charlesworth has also shown that image of the Nehushtan or the serpent in the Temple that Hezekiah and Josiah supposedly removed during their reforms has been found to be the common motif of the goddess: "The veneration of Nehushtan, the copper serpent in the Temple, may be analogous to the worship of Asherah mentioned in 2 Kings 18:4. She is the goddess associated with the serpent cult in the ancient Near East. She often appears nude holding serpents in one hand or both hands." Charlesworth, *The Good and Evil Serpent,* 345.

In addition, William Dever explains, "It seems clear that originally in

be only focused on Yahweh, the Deuteronomists attempted to make Yahweh the sole deity of the Israelite cult, in a manner that echoed Assyrian cultic practices focused on Aššur as the all-powerful deity.[64]

These central ideological changes were advanced through cultic practices and written propaganda, and they echo both contemporary practical theology and rebranding techniques— though most practical theologians and graphic designers would object to the development and deployment of such a violent ideology. The comparison between contemporary theological and design methods helps to elucidate what happened in the seventh century and why the Hebrew Highland Settlements history has remained hidden for nearly twenty-five hundred years, buried below the surface of the Israelite tradition by the Deuteronomistic texts and traditions. With such a contextual understanding, it should be no surprise, then, to see how the conquest story—as part of the sacred text of Judaism, Christianity, and Islam—has helped to support violent, militaristic, and imperialistic practices. Simply

---

ancient Israel there was a Goddess named 'Asherah,' who was associated with living trees and hilltop forest sanctuaries, and who could sometimes be symbolized by a wooden pole or an image of a tree. This tradition concerning the goddess became anathema in time, however, and was perpetuated only in veiled references in the Hebrew Bible, in later Jewish tradition, and in Jewish and Christian versions of the Hebrew Bible. I have called her 'Asherah Abscondia: but she would come back to life in modern times, resuscitated by archaeology (Chapter IV)." Dever, *Did God Have a Wife?* 102. See also Saul M. Olyan, *Asherah and the Cult of Yahweh in Israel* (Atlanta: Scholars Press, 1988).

[64]Richard Jude Thompson hypothesizes that "the DH and the Deuteronomistic covenant mark the historical transformation of a local Phoenician and Canaanite god and state into a military imperial god and state modeled after the image of the god Aššur and the Neo-Assyrian empire." Richard Jude Thompson, *Terror of the Radiance: Aššur Covenant to Yhwh Covenant* (Fribourg: Academic Press, 2013), 234.

put: the conquest story is doing what it was designed to do.

The issue of the conquest narrative is not whether an Israelite conquest took place but that the story has had a mimetic effect in the real world. A world of genocide has unfolded from the conquest narrative. The violence and genocide in Joshua can be and has been understood as part of the divine will. Examples abound, as discussed earlier, where Christian imperialists used these stories to justify the killing of countless Indigenous Peoples, as occurred in the Americas. Regardless of scholarly understandings of the origins of the Joshua narrative that discount its truthfulness, people read the conquest stories as they are: "History is no longer with us. The narrative remains."[65]

Writing's power is in the world or discourse that becomes possible through the narrative and that unfolds from the text.[66] Because the Bible is a sacred Scripture in Western Christianity, the stories within it are imbued with authority and are harnessed by Christian cultures to effect change. The stories of Israelite conquest in the Hebrew Bible have been used in Western Christian contexts to justify actual historical conquests and genocides. That these texts helped create such a world is of grave concern. The conquest story supports a deadly historical imagination that Western Christian cultures use and have used to justify actual genocide, even if the Israelites themselves never did what the text says they did.[67]

---

[65]Robert Warrior, "Canaanites, Cowboys, and Indians," *Christianity & Crisis* 49, no. 12 (September 11, 1989), 3.

[66]Paul Ricœur, *Essays on Biblical Interpretation* (Philadelphia: Fortress, 1980), 3–4. Ricœur argues that regardless of authorial intent, the world of the text is autonomous and bursts forth regardless of the author's intention.

[67]Sacvan Bercovitch, *The Puritan Origins of the American Self* (New Haven, CT: Yale University Press, 1975), 141; Jantzen, *Violence to Eternity*, 98; Warrior, "Cowboys, Canaanites, and Indians," 3.

Conquest and Christendom

The discourse of the conquest narrative has had a broad ideological afterlife far beyond ancient Judah: temporally, geographically, and culturally. While the seventh-century Deuteronomists never achieved an expanded, unified pan-Israelite state, the conquest narrative has served the expansionist goals of others, particularly of European Western cultures and empires.[68] Alongside the colonial history of Christendom, the conquest narrative can be found as part of the theological matrix that has supported an imagination of domination. European Christians appropriated the Israelite story of conquest and read themselves into the narrative as the Israelites, or God's chosen people entering into ever new promised lands ready for the taking.[69] New lands and new characters refract the roles of the Israelites, Canaanites, and promised land. These stories are malleable; anyone can adopt them and interpret them in such a way to achieve a particular political outcome.[70] "Through the ages, and depending on the historical context, the category 'Canaanite' has appeared to be astonishingly flexible."[71] The Crusades, the conquest of

---

[68]Whatever the intentions or the function of the covenant theme and conquest narratives in their original context, they have become, as Jantzen states, "deeply embroiled in violence, a violence which has shaped the West as it took the narrative of covenant and chosen people to be its own." Jantzen, *Violence to Eternity*, 98.

[69]Grace Jantzen explains that if the biblical stories of covenant and conquest "are read, as they have been repeatedly in Western history, as a factual account, indeed as divine revelation, then it is open to anyone who puts themselves into the position of the chosen ones to do violence to those whom they deem to be excluded. . . . It is an ideology that has had a long afterlife in the history of the West." Jantzen, *Violence to Eternity*, 98.

[70]Schwartz, *Curse of Cain*, 157.

[71]Katell Berthelot, Joseph E. David, and Marc G. Hirshman, eds., *The Gift*

the Americas, and the South African apartheid state are only a few political situations in which the conquest narrative has served imagination, practice, and "pre-established political aims."[72] As these examples attest, the world of the conquest narrative is still unfolding.

Yet the liberating elements of the biblical stories that begin with the Israelite exodus from Egypt have also had a broad life well beyond their ancient context. The stories of both the exodus and conquest have been drawn upon at different times and places for very different and even opposite motives. Domination and oppression, liberation and freedom—these biblical stories ignite contrary extremes.[73] The ethical conundrum present in the biblical texts beats at the heart of these extremes. There is a strong mandate to care for the orphan, the widow, and the oppressed, yet on the other hand is the "other" and the command to utterly decimate them.[74] As it stands now in the biblical text, the exodus narrative concludes in conquest and is also rife with its own violent inconsistencies. Yes, the Israelites are saved from the violent oppression of the Egyptians, but salvation came through the death of the Egyptian firstborns and the Egyptian horses and riders that were thrown into the sea. Throughout Christendom, these stories have been

---

of the Land and the Fate of the Canaanites in Jewish Thought (Oxford: Oxford University Press, 2014), 6.

[72]Schwartz, *Curse of Cain*, 157.

[73]Michael Prior asks, "Does not a consistent reading of the biblical text require the liberating God of the Exodus to become the oppressive God of the occupation of Canaan?" Michael Prior, *The Bible and Colonialism: A Moral Critique* (Sheffield: Sheffield Academic Press, 1997), 43.

[74]Regina Schwartz states that this ethical problem led her to write the book *Curse of Cain*. She argues that those biblical texts concerned with Israelite identity over and against the "other" rather than the ethical mandate are overridden. *Curse of Cain*, xi.

foundational identity-forming narratives.[75] It should be no surprise, then, that they have helped to shape history in both liberating and oppressive ways. History and narrative overlap and inform one another, creating identities and peoples in such a way that the line often blurs between them.[76]

When Europeans first stepped foot onto the soil of the Americas, they saw themselves through the lens of the Israelites entering Canaan. The lands and peoples spread out before them were seen as commodities or obstacles that could be ravaged or discarded at will.[77] In the course of several generations, millions of people were killed or displaced as migrating Europeans plowed their way into lands already teeming with people and myriads of cultures. The Europeans were shaped by a theological imagination of conquest that enabled them to see the Indigenous Peoples as subhuman and in need of Christ

---

[75]Grace Jantzen explains how the larger narrative of covenant between Israel and Yahweh (which includes the conquest) has functioned in the West when these stories are read as a factual account: "But if they [biblical stories of covenant and conquest] are read, as they have been repeatedly in Western history, as a factual account, indeed as divine revelation, then it is open to anyone who puts themselves into the position of the chosen ones to do violence to those whom they deem to be excluded. . . . It is an ideology that has had a long afterlife in the history of the West." Jantzen, *Violence to Eternity*, 98.

[76]Schwartz, *Curse of Cain*, 156.

[77]Hawk explains that by "interpreting Joshua as a compendium of principles and directives had a particular impact on the thinking of those European Christians who established colonies around the globe. Reading Joshua within context of the colonial enterprise forged a powerful conceptual link between Israel's conquest of Canaan in obedience to God and the expansion of Christianity and Christian civilization. The English colonization of North America is a well-documented case in point. The Puritans of New England perceived a strong connection between the biblical story of Israel and their own passage through the waters, liberated form bondage and oppression in corrupted England into a 'new Canaan,' where God would raise them up as a covenant people that would be a light to all the nations of the earth." Hawk, *Joshua in 3D*, xxvi.

and the European version of civilization and salvation. This "diseased Christian imagination" provided justification for killing, raping, and displacing peoples with moral and literal impunity.[78] The European conquest of the Americas was and is the world's worst genocide.[79] To this day the US government refuses to recognize the horrific and ongoing genocide of the Native American peoples. Robert Warrior explains that it is "America's self-image as a 'chosen people,' [that] enables the US to feel no accountability for conducting the worst genocide in the history of the world."[80]

---

[78]Willie James Jennings describes the European Christian imagination as "diseased" in his text, *The Christian Imagination*. Daniel Hawk explains that "Puritan attitudes defaulted readily to a perspective that saw possession of the land and the subjugation of hostile nations as a manifestation of God's work. . . . And discomfort with the extermination of indigenous men, women, and children could be calmed by justifying it as God's destruction of the 'instruments of Satan.'" Hawk, *Joshua in 3D*, xxvi–vii. Here Hawk draws on Charles M. Segal and David C. Steinback, *Puritans, Indians, and Manifest Destiny* (New York: Putnam, 1977). Similarly, Sacvan Bercovitch shows how a Puritan ideology enabled the colonists to view the extermination of American Indians with impunity. He argues that the "Puritans, despite their missionary pretenses, regarded the country as theirs and its natives as an obstacle to their destiny as Americans. They could remove that obstacle either by conversion (followed by 'confinement'), or else by extermination. Since the former course proved insecure, they had recourse to the latter." Bercovitch, *The Puritan Origins of the American Self*, 141.

[79]David E. Stannard explains that "within no more than a handful of generations following their first encounters with Europeans, the vast majority of the Western Hemisphere's native peoples had been exterminated. The pace and magnitude of their obliteration varied from place to place and from time to time, but for years now historical demographers have been uncovering, in region upon region, post-Columbian depopulation rates of between 90 and 98 percent with such regularity that an overall decline of 95 percent has become a working rule of thumb. . . . The destruction of the Indians of the Americas was, far and away, the most massive act of genocide in the history of the world." Stannard, *American Holocaust: The Conquest of the New World* (Cary, NC: Oxford University Press, 1993), x.

[80]Warrior, "Canaanites, Cowboys, and Indians," 3.

Additionally, further back in history, the eleventh-century European Christian Crusades were empowered by a xenophobic theology that perpetuated that idea that Jerusalem and the Holy Land should be liberated from "unclean races."[81] This was also an anti-Semitic crusade, as many Jews were killed along the Crusaders' routes to Palestine: "religious idealism led to the attackers' failure to distinguish between the Muslim and the Jewish 'enemy' . . . The same Christian impulse to cleanse the Holy Land from Muslims drove Christians to attack the Jews at home."[82]

Centuries later, South African nationalist myths of origins invoked the exodus and conquest stories as a means to identify Afrikaners with the ancient Israelites who had escaped Egypt (the British) and wandered to the promised land that was filled with Canaanites (Indigenous Africans).[83] This biblical theological underpinning helped to justify the South African apartheid state and ongoing racial oppression and discrimination.

The conquest narrative has also been leveraged in the present-day oppression and displacement of Palestinian people in Israel and the West Bank.[84] In Israel, biblical themes found in the conquest narrative support a nationalistic origins myth that assumes God has given the Jewish people the land of their ancestors by divine right.[85] In addition, Christian Zionists around the globe have supported Israel's right to this land regardless of the death, destruction, and displacement

---

[81]Prior, *Bible and Colonialism*, 35.

[82]Shmuel Shepkaru, "The Preaching of the First Crusade and the Persecutions of the Jews," *Medieval Encounters* 18, no. 1 (January 1, 2012): 96–97.

[83]Prior, *Bible and Colonialism*, 92.

[84]Prior, *Bible and Colonialism*, 39.

[85]Raheb, *Faith in the Face of Empire* (Maryknoll, NY: Orbis Books, 2014), 65.

of the indigenous Palestinians. However, such a view has not been the only Jewish view on the settlement in Palestine. For example, the Rabbi Reines held the position that "it is a divine commandment to settle the land, in the present as in the past, but, in opposition to the time of Joshua and David, the settlement must be done only by peaceful means, such as purchasing land, for God has now forbidden conquest of the land 'with a strong hand.'"[86] There is not only one Jewish perspective on this matter.

It is also important to make a distinction between European colonization of the Americas and the Jewish domination of Palestine, even though they are often listed as equivalents when such discussions occur.[87] Jewish people who left Europe after the Holocaust were not the same as European colonialists. Rather, "the overwhelming number of Jews who founded the modern state had been kicked out of their homelands, and themselves were 'decimated.'. . . Jews were not colonialists who were plundering the Americas or Africa to enrich their home state. There was no welcoming home state."[88] This is an important nuance in accounting for the difference in contexts between Israel and European colonizing projects, especially when anti-Semitism is so prevalent in insidious ways. Differences in these details can be maintained while

---

[86]Katell Berthelot, Joseph E. David, and Marc G. Hirshman, eds., *The Gift of the Land and the Fate of the Canaanites in Jewish Thought* (Oxford: Oxford University Press, 2014), 9. This book is an excellent resource with a variety of Jewish scholars reflecting on the topic of how the conquest narrative has been interpreted in Jewish thought.

[87]Prior, *Bible and Colonialism*, 39. Here, in a quote from Arnold Toynbee, Prior lists as equivalent the Israel conquest of Palestine alongside British colonial projects.

[88]Susan Schnur, from a personal email correspondence discussing the manuscript, June 26, 2022. I am grateful to Dr. Schnur for her feedback on my draft manuscript.

still critiquing Israelite aggression and working for justice for the Palestinians.

The call to care for the widow, the orphan, and the least of these is not heard over the thunderous biblical story of conquest. Those who hold the Bible as sacred text are accountable to the violence wrought in biblical stories unless they do something to undo the power of conquest.

Conclusion

The conquest narrative is an example of the power of the written word. The conquest story literally helped to shape the world in the vision of the conquerors. Over twenty-five hundred years after the conquest narrative was written, we are still faced with the power of the written word and media campaigns designed to perpetuate particular agendas. For example, social media disinformation campaigns are currently destabilizing the US population, perpetuated in part by opportunistic autocratic US leaders and groups as well as foreign powers like Russia. While a large part of the US population is pushing to evolve unjust institutions to become more fully inclusive, another part is actively seeking to solidify an autocratic minority rule that will destroy democracy. Disinformation campaigns abound, seeking to perpetuate a culture war that divides neighbors, families, and states in the United States. Storytelling is at the heart of this cultural moment, just as it was twenty-five hundred years ago during the Josianic kingdom in Judah. The Deuteronomists utilized texts and stories in manipulative ways, writing into history the world they hoped to build in their seventh-century context, faking a book-find to give their new texts "ancient" authority, and allowing these texts to become the foundation for extreme reforms.

Pay attention to our current situation in the United States, and you can see a similar playbook: the attack on history as critical race theory is declared illegal to be taught in schools in many states; targeted social media campaigns support antidemocratic politicians and policies cloaked as constitutional and democratic when really the opposite is the case; reforms based on false information such as the "Big Lie" that the 2020 presidential election was stolen, leading to a series of state election legislative reforms that will result in voter suppression among minority peoples; evangelical and conservative Christian denominations supporting autocratic, neoliberal politicians in exchange for legislation and judicial appointments that back regressive social and reproductive policies. Religion, politics, history, media, and reforms all echo the seventh-century Judean context that produced the Deuteronomistic History and Josianic reforms. It should be no surprise that the conquest narrative itself shows up in the propaganda of the concerted insurrectionist movement in the United States. The so-called Jericho March, one of the organizing marches in Washington, DC, during the January 6, 2021, insurrection, leveraged the Jericho story from the book of Joshua to shape imagination surrounding the insurrectionist movement.[89]

I draw this parallel between current events and seventh-century Judah to illustrate that human cultures are still dealing with the manipulative power of texts, stories, and histories. History repeats itself until we can break the cycles of oppressive behavioral patterns. The Josianic reign is a window into the past that illustrates that cultures have been dealing with this problem since the dawn of the written word.

The Hebrew Bible was written in a transitional period,

---

[89]Emma Green, "A Christian Insurrection," *The Atlantic*, January 8, 2021.

when writing existed only among an elite, scribal class and when most ancient Israelites only had an awareness of written texts while still being deeply embedded within an oral culture.[90] In this transitional period, texts had a special respect and aura surrounding them that linked them "to the realm of the supernatural, its capacity to effect transformation, its magical properties and power."[91] This magical attitude applied to written texts within transitional oral cultures, giving power to the written text. In this context, writing is special, otherworldly, and authoritative.[92] As such, those with the power to produce written texts could exploit this attitude. Draper argues that "legal texts revealed by the gods served to cement and legitimate the power of the ruling elite."[93] If texts were deemed magical, then "sacred" writing could be considered dictation or messages from the gods. In this way, what we might consider "religious" or "sacred" texts can play a distinct propaganda role.[94]

---

[90]See Susan Niditch, *Oral World and Written Word: Ancient Israelite Literature*, Library of Ancient Israel (Louisville, KY: Westminster/John Knox, 1996).

[91]Niditch, *Oral World and Written Word*, 79.

[92]It is interesting to note that even the English term "authority" is etymologically connected to the written text derived from the old French, *auctorité*, meaning "book or quotation that settles an argument." *Online Etymology Dictionary*, s.v. "authority," accessed April 17, 2014, http://www.etymonline.com/index.php?term=authority&allowed_in_frame=0.

[93]Jonathan A. Draper, ed., *Orality, Literacy, and Colonialism in Antiquity*, Society of Biblical Literature Semeia Studies 47 (Atlanta: Society of Biblical Literature, 2004), 1.

[94]Giddens explains the particular power that writing engenders in the ability to construct or create a particular history: "In so far as texts describe 'what went on' plus 'what should go on' in a range of social situations, the 'history' that is written can form a consolidated part of the apparatus of power. What were once a series of customary forms of conduct, informally sanctioned in the daily practices of local communities, become in some part appropriated and administered by the state apparatus. Knowledge of 'history' becomes an interpretive device whereby separate 'authorities' can define what used to be

The twenty-first century CE is vastly different than Judah in the seventh century BCE for myriad reasons, especially in that it is far removed from oral cultures, and we are a literate culture, where the written word is ubiquitous. Though the written word is not a new phenomenon, a media transition is occurring today with the rise of social media.[95] Social media can engender a new tribalism as newsfeeds are manipulated to shape popular opinion and political outcomes. The problems of propaganda and media being used as tools to advance the agendas of those seeking power remain similar to what occurred during the Josianic reforms. Such media problems are not new, having occurred since the advent of sacred texts themselves.

---

controlled by local custom. 'Authority' has a double sense which accurately expresses this, because it is possible to be both an authority on a given sphere of knowledge, and to have authority over others. In the manner described here the two coincide." Anthony Giddens, *The Nation-State and Violence* (Berkeley, CA: University of California Press, 1987), 45.

[95]Technological change in communications practices can have diverse implications regarding transformation of cultural practices and ideologies. See discussion in Mogens Trolle Larsen, *Introduction to Literacy and Society*, ed. K. Schousboe and M. T. Larsen (Copenhagen: Akademisk Forlag, 1989), 7–10. For a broader discussion, also see Brian Street, *Literacy in Theory and Practice* (Cambridge: Cambridge University Press, 1984).

4

Telling the Settlements Story

The Highland Settlements history is a liberating counter-history. Counterhistories read against the grain of dominant histories and challenge dominant forms of knowledge and power.[1] Counterhistories reveal the power of history in the present. A liberating counterhistory points to the ways that a vision of history can replace violent, genocidal visions. For the Highland Settlements, this liberating counterhistory subverts the vision of Israelite history in the conquest narrative. It is likely that the Highland Settlers held some sort of democratic, communitarian, or even utopic ethos.[2] For these reasons, the

---

[1]See Introduction note 20.

[2]Frank Moore Cross, "Reuben, First-Born of Jacob," *Zeitschrift für die alttestamentliche Wissenschaft* 100, no. 3 (1988): 62; William G. Dever, *Who Were the Early Israelites and Where Did They Come From?* (Grand Rapids: Eerdmans, 2003), 249; Avraham Faust, *Israel's Ethnogenesis: Settlement, Interaction, Expansion and Resistance*, Approaches to Anthropological Archaeology (London: Equinox, 2006), 98–99, 105; Gerhard Lenski, "*The Tribes of Yahweh: A Sociology of the Religion of Liberated Israel, 1250–1050 B.C.E.* by Norman K. Gottwald," *Religious Studies Review* 6, no. 4 (October 1980): 275–78; Mario Liverani, *Israel's History and the History of Israel* (London: Routledge, 2014), 67–68.

Highland Settlements can be interpreted as liberative within their Iron Age I context, contrasting the highly stratified Canaanite societies that contained stark divisions between various classes and social and political groups.[3]

Moreover, the Highland Settlements can be interpreted as a liberating counterhistory from a feminist theological perspective. Feminist visions for just societies typically include models of nonhierarchical organization and leadership, guided by an ethic that supports the flourishing of all its members. Such feminist visions stand in contrast to violent and imperialistic societies that are built around a hierarchical leadership model and social strata, which values certain people over others, and typically shows little regard for nature or the environment.[4] While it would be anachronistic to infer that the Highland Settlements were self-consciously feminist as the term is used today, the social organization in the settlements does, in part, reflect societal practices for which contemporary feminist visions advocate. The Highland Settlements echo a feminist pattern of social organization in that they were likely heterarchical or even somewhat egalitarian and practiced more just living conditions in contrast to the oppressive imperial status quo found in the Canaanite cities.

By claiming that the Highland Settlements are a liberating counterhistory, I do not mean that the settlements provide "blueprints" of communities that can straightforwardly offer

---

[3] Avraham Faust, "The Emergence of Iron Age Israel: On Origins and Habitus," in *Israel's Exodus in Transdisciplinary Perspective*, ed. T. Levy, T. Schneider, and W. Propp, Quantitative Methods in the Humanities and Social Sciences (Cham: Springer, 2015), 469.

[4] Feminist concepts of flourishing, natality, and necrophilia come from Grace Jantzen, *Becoming Divine: Toward a Feminist Philosophy of Religion* (Bloomington: Indiana University Press, 1999); Grace M. Jantzen, *Violence to Eternity*, ed. Jeremy Carrette and Morny Joy (London: Routledge, 2009).

guidance for how to live life today.[5] Iron Age I life in Canaan was difficult and harsh by contemporary standards, and I do not advocate mimicking such conditions. Rather, their story can be inspirational to spark imagination for social practices today that reflect the contours of their story.

While we cannot definitively know what life was like in the Highland Settlements, the lack of exact knowledge does not detract from the potential impact of the settlements as an influential counterhistory. Counterhistories do not have to be lengthy, written, or even contain precise details. Rather, counterhistories provide sketches for another way of imagining the past and, therefore, the future.[6] Exact and clear details are not always necessary for counterhistories to disrupt the status quo because they "materialize from emotions and sights and sounds and touch and smell. They come from the deepest part of who we are."[7] As such, the liberative possibilities contained within the Highland Settlements research is not dependent upon precise details. The archaeological evidence provides a historical sketch that reads against the grain of dominant history found in the conquest narrative. It is an alternative sketch of history that can "[jolt] us out of our complacency, and requires us to consider again how past, present, and future are intertwined."[8]

---

[5]For a description of the differences between genres of utopia, including blueprint utopias that offer a specific design of action to be taken to create a perfect society, see Erin McKenna, *The Task of Utopia: A Pragmatist and Feminist Perspective* (Lanham, MD: Rowman & Littlefield, 2002).

[6]Graham, "A Remembrance of Things (Best) Forgotten," 12.

[7]Townes, *Womanist Ethics and the Cultural Production of Evil,* 45–46. Here Townes describes the essence of social change possible through what she calls countermemories. Her ideas of countermemories are similar to the concept of counterhistory and so I draw on her work on countermemory in this conversation as well.

[8]Graham, "A Remembrance of Things (Best) Forgotten," 12. Here Graham

The Highland Settlements historical sketch provides the contours of an exodus story of sorts reminiscent of the biblical exodus and other stories in popular imagination. Following the indigenous origins theory of interpretation, the Highland Settlements material tells of oppressed people and social dissidents who left oppressive city-states and went to the highland frontier for "a new beginning."[9] Their history parallels popular folklore in Western culture like Robin Hood and his band of merry men in Sherwood Forest, tapping into an archetype of common people living on the edges of empire.

The Highland Settlements history resonates with people's emotions today because its cultural and ecological context echoes contemporary conditions. Current problems of extreme socioeconomic injustice and climate change are reflected in the Highland Settlements story. Understanding how the Highland Settlers responded to similar hardships can inspire people today, especially as their story is at the root of three major religious traditions that billions of people now practice. The Highland Settlers leveraged new, democratizing technologies of their day to aid in the building of more just communities. Many justice-seeking churches are doing similar types of innovative praxis that leverage today's technologies. The Highland Settlements history grounds such innovative community building within the very roots of the biblical tradition, providing a deep-seated legitimacy to such practices.

---

refers specifically to the TV show *Mad Men*, but she is also making a broader argument about counterhistories in general.

[9]William G. Dever, *Beyond the Texts: An Archaeological Portrait of Ancient Israel and Judah* (Atlanta: SBL Press, 2017), 226.

Golden Age?

Upholding the Highland Settlements as a liberating counterhistory does not mean that they should be idealized or canonized as some sort of lost golden age.[10] A nuanced approach is needed.[11] The Highland Settlements were not utopias, but they can be understood as a liberative social movement in their time. They can be looked to for inspiration and celebrated in contemporary biblical faith communities without creating an idol of them.

Norman Gottwald recognized that the egalitarian vision of ancient Israel that he first put forward in *The Tribes of Yahweh* is a far more complex social reality than the term "egalitarian" conveys, but he still contended that something akin to the utopic did occur in ancient Israel. He tempers his understanding of the utopic with a full understanding that the standard of life in the Iron Age was low and filled with considerable bloodshed, and he warns against romanticizing ancient Israel as "an ideal golden age."[12] Still, the archaeological evidence, like pottery and the foundations of build-

---

[10]Gottwald warns against idolizing or canonizing *Tribes* without an awareness of its "errors and shortcomings." Norman K. Gottwald, "Political Activism and Biblical Scholarship: An Interview," in *Tracking* The Tribes of Yahweh: *On the Trail of a Classic*, ed. Roland Boer (London: Sheffield Academic, 2002), 181.

[11]David Jobling, "Specters of *Tribes*: On the 'Revenance' of a Classic," in *Tracking* The Tribes of Yahweh, 15.

[12]Gottwald states that "such a day of justice [utopia] was approximated in ancient Israel, whatever the social organizational label we give it. . . . This can be grasped without treasuring it romantically as an ideal golden age. In Israel's tribal society, the standard of living was low, the culture options minimal, the internecine bickering and bloodshed considerable." Gottwald, " 'Political Activism and Biblical Scholarship: An Interview,' " 183.

ings and settlements, can nevertheless prompt questions now that inspire imagination and actions. Gottwald explains that, because ancient Israel is "lodged" in the memory of the three biblical traditions, the Highland Settlements are not a random or "rootless utopia" but are part of our history.[13] Historical utopias can inspire new possibilities for our own contexts and raise questions such as, What do "peace and justice require of us in a situation of technological and social complexity with outmoded political organization overrun by the juggernaut of economic globalization"?[14] Biblical scholar David Jobling notes that while biblical studies has complicated the idea of a simplistic understanding of Israelite history as egalitarian, nevertheless an "egalitarian presence" does appear in biblical texts.[15] Jobling understands the importance of people connecting a vision of an egalitarian Israel with liberative praxis. He states that he does not correct people when he witnesses them making this connection without nuance, because as he asks, Why discourage people's interpretations of ancient Israel just because they are not as nuanced as scholars, if their interpretations are prompting liberative praxis?[16]

Feminist theology, in part, emphasizes the importance of liberative histories, so as I first learned about the Highland Settlements, as a feminist practical theologian I was already attuned to notice the utopic quality of the Highland Settlements and, in turn, to ask how they might inspire liberative praxis today. How the Highland Settlements archaeological research can prompt utopic imagination and practice in contemporary

---

[13]Gottwald, "Response to Contributors," in *Tracking* The Tribes of Yahweh, 182–84.

[14]Gottwald, " 'Political Activism and Biblical Scholarship: An Interview,'" 183.

[15]Jobling, "Specters of *Tribes*," 14.

[16]Jobling, "Specters of *Tribes*, 15.

ecclesiology is a practical theological question. Gottwald himself raises a very practical question, asking why and how we can link the Highland Settlements with justice-seeking ecclesial and secular communities.[17] He speculates that the reason we link the Highland Settlements with contemporary communities is early Israel's connection to the biblical traditions, but he does not speculate on how we might link these ancient communities with contemporary ecclesial and secular communities.[18] Since the disciplines of biblical studies and practical theology have very different methods and aims, it is not surprising that Gottwald and other biblical scholars have not taken up the *how* question that Gottwald raises, because it is a practical theological concern. Answering how the Highland Settlements research can transform Christian faith practice is, however, suited to feminist practical theology, since a rich strand in feminist discourse explores how liberative and even utopic historical research can help to transform the present.

Liberating Imagination

The Highland Settlements counterhistory is already shaping a liberative and radical imagination. As discussed briefly in chapter 1, some biblical scholars find that teaching about the Highland Settlements prompts inspiration, excitement, and a desire for additional knowledge across a variety of contexts—a "*Tribes* moment."[19] Norman Gottwald reported that one of

---

[17]Gottwald, "Response to Contributors," 184.

[18]Gottwald, "Response to Contributors," 184.

[19]The name "*Tribes* moment" to describe the inspiration people feel learning about the Highland Settlements is in reference to Norman Gottwald's book *The Tribes of Yahweh: A Sociology of the Religion of Liberated Israel, 1250–1050 B.C.* (Maryknoll, NY: Orbis Books, 1979), which ended up bringing forward to

his biggest surprises in writing *The Tribes of Yahweh* was the number of people outside of academic circles who read the book, including clergy, lay intellectuals, and social justice activists around the world.[20] Gottwald likewise describes how *Tribes* influenced political activists around the globe, including South African graduate students in theology, imprisoned for activist work, who took a copy of *Tribes* into prison as their "holy book," passing it back and forth between cells so all could read it.[21] Gottwald's stories attest to how interpretations of the Highland Settlements counterhistory inspire students and people engaged in justice issues around the globe, even while imprisoned.

In my own experience, when I share research on the Highland Settlements with people across differing theological perspectives (ranging from biblical literalists to mainline progressives to those who identify as spiritual but not religious), I find most are captivated by the story and ask questions like, How have I not learned this before? Why aren't churches talking about this? Where do I find out more? During my own *Tribes* moment, I was stunned and wondered why I had never heard this historical information in the churches I grew up in, which cared very much about Israel and biblical history.[22]

---

a broad audience the Highland Settlements archaeological evidence. Jobling, "Specters of *Tribes*," 15.

[20]In addition to the aforementioned Colombian Catholic nuns and South Korean scholar and political prisoner, Gottwald tells of an African American junior high teacher in New Jersey who taught *Tribes* to a "spell-bound" group of kids and a graduate student who wrote him a thank-you note for bringing forward such a powerful historical reconstruction. Gottwald, "Response to Contributors," 181.

[21]Gottwald, " 'Political Activism and Biblical Scholarship: An Interview,' " 166–67.

[22]The following several texts contributed to my own *Tribes* moment: Israel Finkelstein and Neil Asher Silberman, *The Bible Unearthed: Archaeology's New Vision of Ancient Israel and the Origin of Its Sacred Texts* (New York:

Students also ask what they can do with the Highland Settlements information. After a lecture I gave interpreting the Highland Settlements as a resource for contemporary ministry practices, a student commented that he was excited to hear the information connected to contemporary contexts. When he first learned of the Highland Settlements research in a Hebrew Bible course, he felt "left in the mud," because the research upended much of what he thought he knew about the Bible, and he did not know what to do with the new story.[23] He wondered what the story meant theologically or for the church.

The student's experience points to the intertwined challenges the Highland Settlements pose for theology, understanding the Bible, and for church praxis. He was initially moved by the Highland Settlements research but did not know how to integrate the theological and biblical challenges inherently posed by the new information within his own faith and ministry practice. Engaging these challenges is at the heart of *Undoing Conquest*.

Storying the Settlements

Part of the challenge of integrating the Highland Settlements information into Christian practice is that the story is contained within archaeological and biblical studies discourses. The Highland Settlements information sheds light on Hebrew origins and connects with certain biblical stories but it

---

Simon and Schuster, 2002); Gottwald, *The Tribes of Yahweh*; Mario Liverani, *Israel's History and the History of Israel* (London: Routledge, 2014); Keith W. Whitelam, *The Invention of Ancient Israel: The Silencing of Palestinian History*, Ancient Near East, Biblical Studies (London: Routledge, 2003).

[23]Shared with permission from Rev. Justin McCall, a student at Methodist Theological School in Ohio at the time.

is told through academic media. For the Highland Settlements data to become truly integrated into faith communities, the archaeological evidence needs to be *storied*. By "storied," I mean that a key step to theologically integrating the Highland Settlements into the life of the church is to communicate the essence of the settlements evidence and its integral connection with Israelite history and certain biblical texts into poetic language or a story that is memorable, symbolic, and accessible to liturgical practice. The act of storying the Highland Settlements is a theopoetic practical theological task.[24]

Fortunately, the foundational biblical story of the exodus already contains an integral connection with the Highland Settlements history. Scholars have noticed that the historical contours of the Highland Settlements research provides an outline of an exodus of sorts reminiscent of the biblical exodus story. Storying the Highland Settlements history need not require crafting a new story but can draw on the existing motif of the exodus narrative to wrap the Highland Settlements evidence in a story that rests at the heart of the Bible and the biblical faith traditions.

The Exodus as Cultural Memory

As discussed briefly in chapter 2, but in more detail here, from a cultural memory studies perspective, the Israelite story

---

[24]How we speak about theology and the Divine shapes our understanding. Theopoetics discourse calls for the need to utilize language and practices beyond academic theological discourse to communicate theological ideas. The ineffable nature of concepts of the Divine call for greater aesthetic and poetic approaches in theology. This is especially true when considering how to communicate academic theological insights within liturgical spaces. For a foundational theopoetic text, see Amos N. Wilder, *Theopoetic: Theology and the Religious Imagination* (Philadelphia: Fortress, 1976).

of the exodus from Egypt refracts the Highland Settlements period through its basic, albeit abstracted, plotlines: people miraculously leaving oppressive conditions of empire and starting anew.[25] Rather than representing the specific experiences of one group of people enslaved in Egypt, the exodus can be understood as a conflation of a broad set of collective experiences from the settlements period.[26] This leads some scholars to speculate that the exodus story is the earliest source for understanding the cultural and religious worldview of the ancient Israelites.[27]

While the written biblical story in the book of Exodus portrays a geographic understanding of Egypt as the Nile region in northeast Africa, the story need not be read so literally. A Late Bronze Age map of the Egyptian Empire includes Canaan since Egypt controlled this region. Even if most of the Highland Settlers were indigenous Canaanites who left the oppressive conditions of the urban lowlands of Canaan for the rural highlands, they still left Egypt. The story in Exodus makes the events of this period seem much more specific and geographically limited, losing this broader geopolitical mapping of the Egyptian Empire.

Nadav Na'aman argues that the basic Exodus plot repre-

---

[25]Nadav Na'aman, "The Exodus Story: Between Historical Memory and Historiographical Composition," *Journal of Ancient Near Eastern Religions* 11, no. 1 (2011): 68–69.

[26]Nadav Na'aman, "The Exodus Story," 68–69; William H. C. Propp, *Exodus 19–40: A New Translation with Introduction and Commentary* (New York: Doubleday, 2006), 741.

[27]Na'aman also uses a cultural memory studies approach to interpreting the exodus story. Nadav Na'aman, "Out of Egypt or Out of Canaan? The Exodus Story between Memory and Historical Reality," in *Israel's Exodus in Transdisciplinary Perspective: Text, Archaeology, Culture, and Geoscience*, ed. Thomas E. Levy, Thomas Schneider, and William H. C. Propp (Cham: Springer International, 2015), 531.

sents the cultural memory of the Canaanites, who experienced the sudden withdrawal of Egypt from Canaan at the end of the Late Bronze Age after nearly 350 years of subjugation.[28] Egypt's departure meant freedom and liberation for the Canaanite people who lived for centuries under imperial rule. Na'aman argues that eventually the cultural memory of Egypt miraculously leaving Canaan was inverted in the written story, and the main plot became the Israelites leaving Egypt.[29] However, interpreted in a less textually literal way than does Na'aman, the Canaanites did leave Egypt as Exodus depicts. It may not be that the written narrative was inverted, but that the exodus is interpreted too literally in its geography. Egyptian departure from Canaan was not the only movement occurring during the Late Bronze Age and Early Iron Age periods. Many indigenous Canaanites were also on the move. Migrating Canaanites left or came out of Egypt as they chose to move away from Egyptian-controlled city-states and begin a new settlement pattern in the highlands. The Canaanites did indeed leave Egypt even though they never left Canaan.

A cultural memory approach to history—"mnemohistory"—further elucidates Exodus as a narrative that speaks symbolically about the Highland Settlement period. Mnemohistory is a literary reception theory that "is concerned not with the past as such, but only with the past as it is remembered," particularly how groups construct a collective identity by symbolically narrating a multiplicity of past events into one

---

[28]Na'aman, "The Exodus Story," 68–69. Na'aman explains that "the cultural memory of the Exodus as shaped in oral tradition, and later as crystallized in a literary form, has had far-reaching impact on the shaping of Israelite consciousness for all generations to come" (68).

[29]Na'aman states that it is "no wonder that the withdrawal [of Egypt from Canaan] was conceived as a kind of miracle that the local inhabitants attributed to their God." Na'aman, "Out of Egypt or Out of Canaan?," 530.

unified and symbolic story.[30] Ron Hendel draws on mnemo-history to suggest that the exodus story acted as a unifying narrative by drawing together a conglomeration of past events from the Highland Settlements era and melding them into the story of Exodus.[31]

Hendel argues that the Canaanite cultural memory of enslavement emerged through experiences of oppression under Egyptian imperialism in Canaan from the Early to the Late Bronze Age. In this frame, the liberative narrative of Exodus works to make symbolic meaning of experiences that spanned generations. Enslavement, oppression under an unnamed pharaoh, and the dramatic escape from Egypt represent diverse experiences of Egyptian power throughout the Canaanite population and their subsequent escape to the highland region during the settlement time period.[32] Given how shared memories of collective suffering can foster the emergence and deepening of ethnic identities, such disparate and personal narratives could have provided space for a growing sense of solidarity as the descendants of the Canaanite oppressed told their stories.[33] Beginning as an oral origin story of Hebrew emergence that would be written down centuries later, the exodus story fostered a sense of group cohesion that led to a nascent Israelite ethnicity.

Unifying Mythology

Before I encountered the research of Ron Hendel or Nadav Na'aman, I made a similar connection between the Highland

---

[30]Jan Assmann, *Moses the Egyptian: The Memory of Egypt in Western Monotheism* (Cambridge, MA: Harvard University Press, 1997), 9.

[31]See chapter 2, note 117.

[32]See chapter 2, note 118.

[33]See chapter 2, note 119.

Settlements and the exodus story from the perspective of graphic design, in particular the practice of corporate branding.[34] Branding offers another way to understand the interconnection between the exodus story and the Highland Settlements that enriches the cultural memory proposals of Hendel and Na'aman. Taken together, these approaches provide more insight on how the exodus narrative could have operated during this formative period of Israelite ethnogenesis.[35]

After initially studying the Highland Settlements archaeological evidence, I was left pondering a fundamental question: If it was not Yahwism or a shared ethnic identity that united the diverse Iron Age I Highland Settlers, then what unified them? What was their common story? Without Yahwism or a shared ethnic background, the settlers would have needed some common unifying element to bind them together in their communitas and pioneering settlements, especially given that they were a heterogeneous group of people who experienced a steady population increase during the Iron Age I period that cannot be attributed to natural birthrates alone.[36]

Approaching these questions through a graphic design perspective, parallels between the plotline of the exodus story and details of the Highland Settlements evidence—

---

[34]Graphic design not only shapes my strategic practical theological approaches, it also informs my hermeneutical lens and interpretive work in biblical studies. For the theories of Hendel and Na'aman, see chapter 2 as well as Hendel, *Remembering Abraham*, and Na'aman, "Out of Egypt or Out of Canaan?"

[35]I discuss my approach developed from graphic design, because it adds a slightly different perspective than those of Hendel and Na'aman discussed earlier; taken together, these different approaches provide a richer lens of understanding. In that way, I want to name my own process in that it might enrich other perspectives as well.

[36]See chapter 2, note 45.

Egyptian subjugation and Israelite liberation—emerged. Within these parallels, the basic exodus plotline can be understood to function as a unifying mythology in similar ways to how a corporate brand identity attempts to communicate the mythos or story of a business. From a branding perspective, the basic exodus plot provides a unifying metaphor that could speak symbolically to the collective Highland Settlement experience even if the experiences of people within the settlement villages differed. All of the settlers left Egypt in some way or another, and this basic commonality became the foundation of a unifying story of communitas. Just as the Nike brand speaks to a great multitude of athletic apparel across different sports, the exodus story, in its most basic form, could speak to a multitude of different experiences of people leaving places controlled by oppressive Egyptian imperial forces.

By using branding analogously to interpret the exodus narrative as a unifying mythology, I am not suggesting that the Highland Settlers intentionally set out to create a specific story to unite their similar-yet-different experiences in a way that a graphic designer might be hired to do for a business client. It is likely that an oral history emerged quite naturally to explain the dramatic withdrawal of Egypt from Canaan after nearly 350 years of rule in the region.[37] It is easy to imagine that, as each new settler group came to the Highland Settlements, they shared what brought them there: their own experience of exodus from Egypt. I imagine these stories being told again and again around a campfire, slowly and naturally melding into a cohesive narrative that gave a common identity to all those gathered.

---

[37]Na'aman, "The Exodus Story," 64.

The various circumstances under which different Highland
Settlement groups "left" Egypt might lie behind the plagues
that Yahweh causes in the biblical story (Ex 7:14–12:36).
The plagues could represent a compilation of chaotic experiences the Canaanite people endured over the course of many
decades at the end of the Late Bronze Age due to severe
climate change, the invasion of seafaring peoples, and the
collapse of the Egyptian Empire. In this unstable ecological and political context, it is not hard to imagine that some
Highland Settlers may have experienced cataclysmic events
of famine, pestilence, and death as they made the decision
to leave their homes and migrate to the highland regions. It
is also easy to imagine that some Highland Settlers viewed
their escape from Egypt and the subsequent collapse of the
Egyptian empire as miraculous.

Metaphorically speaking, the exodus story points to the historical experience of the Highland Settlers even if the details
of the story are not factually accurate. When the exodus story
is read as a unifying metaphor that provided a sense of shared
identity for diverse groups of Highland Settlers, its narrative
arc shimmers around the details of the archaeological evidence
for the Highland Settlements in an unstable regional context.
As such, the exodus story can be understood as hyperreal;
that is, it is exaggerated in comparison to reality. It depicts
a broad compilation of the Highland Settlers' experiences
leaving Egypt, even if it is not exactly as the story depicts it.

Decoupling Exodus and Conquest

When interpreting Exodus through the perspectives of
cultural memory, mnemohistory, or branding, it is important

to note that there would not be a conquest at the end of a Highland Settlements telling of an exodus story. Archaeological evidence does not connect the conquest story to a cultural memory from the Highland Settlements period, for there is no archaeological evidence of weapons or destruction of Canaanite cities by the settlers. Moreover, the settlement villages were not fortified for any sort of militaristic battles. The Hebrew houses were arranged to keep children and pastoral animals in and wild animals and human intruders out, but not in such a way to stop a militaristic advance. Rather than aligning with the cultural memory of the Highland Settlers, the conquest narrative aligns with the Assyrian-influenced political visions of the seventh-century BCE Judean Deuteronomists.

Because the exodus story is a central theme of Judaism and is the most mentioned event in the Bible, it would have been difficult to change the fundamental plotlines of the story to fit seventh-century BCE Judean geopolitical aims when the Deuteronomistic history was being written. So, rather than changing the basic story of Exodus, the Deuteronomist created a new militaristic ending to the story, and, by doing so, reshaped Israelite history.[38] The exodus story remained intact, but its liberative storyline was undermined by a genocidal ending.[39]

---

[38]Here I follow feminist hermeneutical approaches to the New Testament from Elisabeth Schüssler Fiorenza, who argues that the women mentioned in the New Testament must have been so prominent in the early Christian traditions that later patriarchal redactions could not completely remove these women from the texts or fully erase their memory. See Elisabeth Schüssler Fiorenza, *In Memory of Her: A Feminist Theological Reconstruction of Christian Origins*, 10th ann. ed. (New York: Crossroad, 1994).

[39]To be sure, violence and death are a part of the exodus story as well when considering the death of the Egyptian firstborn children and the drowning of the Egyptian army in the sea. The Exodus is not a nonviolent story.

The exodus is not, however, a nonviolent story. The narrative contains problematic violence that can undermine its liberative qualities. Indeed, the exodus includes the mass destruction of the plagues, the killing of the Egyptian firstborns, and the drowning of the Egyptian army. A womanist reading of Exodus calls out the divine violence against the Egyptians, including the premeditated and sacrificial murder of the firstborn Egyptians.[40] Cheryl Kirk-Duggan argues that Exodus must challenge this horrific bloodshed and questions interpretations that deem this violent injustice against the Egyptians as righteousness.[41] Divinely sanctioned violence is not a healthy answer for injustice, and more nuanced approaches are needed, such as conflict resolution, mediation, and negotiation.[42]

Laurel Dykstra finds Exodus disturbingly violent but thinks that the violence in these stories can help contemporary readers address structural violence in their own culture.[43] She asks first-world Christians to read Exodus and identify with the Egyptians, to face the hard truths of how "we serve the empire of global capitalism. Like Egypt, we are complicit

---

However, this violence is carried out by Yahweh in a miraculous and divine manner, and decidedly not by the oppressed people themselves in a systematic military campaign that reflects the conquest of other imperial powers like the Assyrian Empire. More will be said on the violence in the exodus story in the next section.

[40]Cheryl A. Kirk-Duggan, "How Liberating Is the Exodus and for Whom?: Deconstructing Exodus Motifs in Scripture, Literature, and Life," in *Exodus and Deuteronomy*, ed. Gale A. Yee and Athalya Brenner (Minneapolis: Fortress Press, 2012), 3.

[41]Kirk-Duggan, "How Liberating Is the Exodus and for Whom?," 20. As she explains, "We cannot let tradition and faith allow us to read these texts uncritically and go with the adage that 'God is on our side,' at any cost."

[42]Kirk-Duggan, "How Liberating Is the Exodus and for Whom?," 21.

[43]Laurel Dykstra, *Set Them Free: The Other Side of Exodus* (Maryknoll, NY: Orbis, 2002), 196.

in oppression, slavery, and genocide. Facing these truths is the beginning of true conversion."[44] I am less confident that Dykstra's hermeneutical approach is the best way to deal with violent texts—in this case, asking privileged people to read Exodus from the perspective of the Egyptians.[45] While this may be a good strategy in certain contexts where people are open to self-reflection, her strategy does not deal directly with the social imaginary that can be built from the violence in these stories. While Dykstra's hermeneutical approach has liberative possibilities, more is needed to ensure that the violence in the exodus and conquest stories do not once again justify atrocities done in the name of the church. Another strategy is to decouple the exodus from the conquest, centering the liberative, egalitarian, and even utopic story of the Highland Settlements as the origins of the Israelite and subsequent biblical traditions and highlighting its connection to Exodus.

Liberating Exodus

Within the Bible, the exodus and conquest stories are edited together into a narrative portmanteau: they are two different stories that explain Hebrew origins in Canaan but are woven

---

[44]Dykstra, *Set Them Free*, 213.

[45]Here I follow the arguments of Melanie May, Laurie Hersh, and Ivone Gebara, who argue that hermeneutical approaches are not always enough when it comes to dealing with violent scriptural texts. See Ivone Gebara, "A Feminist Theology of Liberation: A Latin American Perspective with a View Toward the Future," in *Hope Abundant: Third World and Indigenous Women's Theology* (Maryknoll, NY: Orbis, 2010), 59; Melanie A. May and Lauree Hersch, "Unity of the Bible, Unity of the Church: Confessionalism, Ecumenism, and Feminist Hermeneutics," in *Searching the Scriptures*, vol. 1 (New York: Crossroad, 1997), 148.

into one. Striking differences in the stories are underscored in the ways in which violence is imagined in Exodus in contrast to the ways violence is imagined in Joshua. The violence of Exodus is ascribed to Yahweh, whereas the violence in Joshua is done by the Israelites, albeit directed by Yahweh. There is seemingly miraculous and divine violence found in Exodus that contrasts with the systematic military conquest promulgated by the Israelites (that closely mirrors Assyrian imperial campaigns) found in Joshua. This is not to say that divine violence is commendable, but rather the ways of understanding violence and its justification vary greatly between the two stories. For example, Yahweh condones the mass genocide of the *herem* in Joshua, whereas in Exodus the Hebrew people question the violence of Moses when he kills the slave driver (Ex 2:11–14). They ask Moses, who challenges them to stop fighting: "Who made you a ruler and judge over us? Do you mean to kill me as you killed the Egyptian?" (Ex 2:14a). Why should the murder of one Egyptian be a problem when the future Israelites will murder entire inhabitants of Canaanite towns, according to the book of Joshua? Such differences can be traced to the contexts from which the stories are developed: the early Iron Age Highland Settlements and the seventh-century political class in Judah.

Though the exodus and conquest read as a singular narrative in the Bible, they come from different times with different ideological perspectives. The archaeological and biblical studies research of the last century now makes possible an interpretive decoupling of the exodus and conquest. The stories can be separated and contextualized within different eras and no longer taken for granted as a singular history. Severing this narrative portmanteau liberates the exodus from conquest. The exodus story no longer needs to end in conquest. Exodus can stand on its own as the miraculous story of the Hebrew people's escape from Egypt and the start of something new.

The Power of Exodus

Exodus is one of the most recognized books of the Bible. Within the Bible itself, the exodus is the most mentioned event and is discussed in all the different genres of the Hebrew Bible: poetry, law, historiography, prophecy, and the Psalms all contain reference to the exodus event.[46] It is a central story in ritual practices of Judaism, such as the Passover seder. Outside the pages of the Bible, the exodus story has inspired liberation and social justice movements around the globe, like the civil rights movement in the United States.[47] The exodus is also prominent in Western popular culture more broadly. US films such as the classic Cecil B. DeMille film *The Ten Commandments* (1958) or the Dreamworks Animation feature film *The Prince of Egypt* (1998) attest to the wide cultural appeal of the exodus and its prominent place in Western social imaginaries. As such, the exodus story has far-reaching religious and cultural appeal.

The exodus connects the Highland Settlements to the biblical traditions, which is important if a new history is to have an impact on radical imagination. In order for the current symbol system to prompt radical imagination, new images must

---

[46]Na'aman, "The Exodus Story," 39.

[47]Kenyatta R. Gilbert, *Exodus Preaching: Crafting Sermons about Justice and Hope* (Nashville: Abingdon, 2018); Gary S. Selby, *Martin Luther King and the Rhetoric of Freedom: The Exodus Narrative in America's Struggle for Civil Rights*, Studies in Rhetoric and Religion 5 (Waco, TX: Baylor University Press, 2008); Rhondda Robinson Thomas, *Claiming Exodus: A Cultural History of Afro-Atlantic Identity, 1774–1903* (Waco, TX: Baylor University Press, 2013).

emerge from within it. Connecting the Highland Settlements with the exodus is a powerful, symbolic, and memorable approach to storying the Highland Settlements in a manner that is accessible to liturgies and faith communities. A cultural memory retelling of the exodus story creates an opportunity to craft a nonviolent understanding of the exodus that follows the Highland Settlements archaeological evidence and describes peaceful cohabitation of diverse groups of people and the building of new communities.[48] Such a telling brings forth the liberating aspects of the exodus while leaving behind the problematic violent details found in the biblical story. The biblical story of the exodus can come to life in a new way.

It is already a common strategy to draw on symbolic themes from the exodus to communicate liberation motifs in varying contexts. For example, Martin Luther King Jr. often leveraged exodus themes in his speeches, and African Americans utilized exodus metaphors to frame their own suffering and fight for liberation during enslavement in the United States. The exodus also inspired many liberation movements, including Latin American liberation theologies and the abolitionist movement in the United States. The liberative metaphoric appeal of the biblical exodus story clearly extends beyond the pages of the Bible.

As such, the symbolism of the exodus story is an excellent vehicle to help communicate the Highland Settlements counterhistory in a way that is already familiar to many people.[49]

---

[48]I call the early settlements peaceful because of the likely egalitarian or even utopic ideals the early settlers were thought to hold and also for their general lack of weapons or fortification of the villages. See Faust, *Israel's Ethnogenesis*, 95–107. In a section titled "Israel's Egalitarian Ethos—Summary of Previous Research," Faust provides an excellent discussion of different scholars' view on the topic of an egalitarian ethos of the Highland Settlements.

[49]The connection between interpreting the exodus story as a mnemo-

There is no need to reinvent the wheel when imagining a way to symbolically communicate the Highland Settlements material when a powerful story with real connections to the history of the settlements already exists in the exodus story.

Theopoetic Storying of the Highland Settlements

For the Highland Settlements to inspire religious imagination, their story must be told. Social imagination is constructed from the stories—the myths, symbols, and narratives—that cultures tell.[50] Therefore, to shape religious imagination, the Highland Settlements evidence will need to be incorporated into the Christian tradition and become a prominent part of Christian identity. For this to happen, churches cannot simply communicate the Highland Settlements material peripherally through a few sermons or a study group. To be fully incorporated into the Christian tradition, the Highland Settlements story must be told frequently. What is more, it will not be sufficient for churches to share the Highland Settlements information only through archaeology and biblical studies research, though these are important. To reshape Christian imagination, more effective forms of communication are needed. How the story is told is as important as the story itself.

Graphic design demonstrates the need for a symbolic communication of the settlements story that can be integrated and communicated across media. Like a logo or another element of a brand, a symbolic communication of the Highland Settle-

---

history or cultural memory of the Highland Settlements people has already been discussed in chapter 3.

[50]Charles Taylor, *Modern Social Imaginaries*, Public Planet Books (Durham, NC: Duke University Press, 2004), 23.

ment material should convey a variety of information about the Highland Settlements research in a medium and language that can be easily integrated into Christian praxis and remembered by those who experience it.

Faith traditions are always evolving, changing, and incorporating new information. Developing a symbolic telling of the Highland Settlements in connections to the biblical story of the exodus directly links the settlements history with the biblical tradition. Without changing the biblical canon, new stories can still be integrated into faith practices. The following narration is one possibility of a symbolic telling of the Highland Settlements story that integrates key themes from the biblical exodus (Ex 1–15:21) with key details of the Highland Settlements archaeological material as interpreted from an indigenous origins theory perspective. Imagine this story being read in a liturgical context:

Exodus to the Highlands

A great exodus occurred around the end of the Bronze Age (c. 1200 BCE) in the land of Canaan. Many people faced oppressive economic situations and even slavery by the Egyptian Empire that cared more for enriching itself than caring for its people. During this time, an unprecedented drought occurred, making the already difficult situation worse. People suffered greatly and cried out for help. Some heard a story that there were new villages, out of reach of the Egyptians, in the rocky highlands. They heard that these new villages were far different from the harsh conditions of the Egyptian Empire. The people heard that this place had no kings who hoarded all the wealth and enslaved the people. People believed this story and went in search of these places.

This was the time of the great exodus. Over the course of many years, people from many different places left their homes to find these new communities. They headed to the hills. Many of the exodus peoples became part of these rocky hillside villages in Canaan. As their numbers grew, they built new villages. They made new tools, built new houses, learned new ways to farm, and dug new wells. They each told their story of escape and exodus. They witnessed from a distance as the once-powerful cities collapsed at the hands of seafaring invaders, famines, and other untold destructions. They could not believe their eyes as they saw the oppressive Egyptian civilization collapse. They agreed it was some sort of miracle.

All the while, they forged new lives: built new communities, made uninhabitable terrain habitable, created a new language. On these rocky hilltops of Canaan, the Hebrew people were born. They were a diverse group of people who shared the resources of the land and created a society with far less socioeconomic divides.

These brave and innovative people are the ancestors of the Israelite people who would go on to develop the biblical traditions. Their spirit enlivens liberation movements around the globe. Now, some three thousand years later, we stand in the shadow of their dream. How can we once again make it come alive? What is our own exodus? How do we become an exodus people?

The Highland Settlements exodus-like narration does not focus on violence—either divine or human—but on the injustices of the Egyptian Empire, climate change, and the Highland Settlers' actions of leaving the empire and starting something new. The symbolic telling is poetic and succinct, which enables easy adaptation into liturgical praxis, to be read as a liturgical prayer or moment of reflection. It could be integrated as a new moment in the weekly worship service, where the origin of the Hebrew tradition is remembered. Just as the Lord's Prayer is recited, the Highland Settlements story could be read as the congregation is invited to listen and reflect. The Highland Settlements story could also become the foundation for children's pageants and plays.

The symbolic storying of the Highland Settlements and these few, quick examples of how churches could incorporate the story into current liturgical practices are only a start. The following chapter details ways that the Highland Settlements research can help to shape theology and praxis within ecclesial and other cultural settings.

Season of Origins

Practices reveal and shape theology. We become what we practice. The Highland Settlements were discovered decades ago, but the practical theological question remains of what to do with this information from a faith community perspective. To incorporate the Highland Settlements into Christian or other faith traditions, the story must be put into practice. The symbolic rendering of the Highland Settlements story in the previous chapter, "Exodus to the Ḥighlands," is one step toward such practical theological work. The remainder of this book takes the work further, developing practices that incorporate the Highland Settlements into the life of the church. I make tangible suggestions for how churches, seminaries, and other interested communities can integrate educational practices, explore biblical scholarship, and reflect theologically on the Highland Settlements. These are starting points, recommendations meant to spark more practical ideas.

Both this chapter and the appendix explore how the Highland Settlements information can challenge, enrich, and shape new perspectives and practices. Some ideas can be implemented right away; some will require more planning. These suggestions are not meant to be prescriptive but are examples meant to inspire. I encourage each community to alter these suggestions or develop novel practices that are relevant and meaningful for them. My hope is that it will also spark different faith traditions—whether Jewish, Muslim, Unitarian Universalist, or others—to develop practices to integrate the Highland Settlements in ways that align with their own theological perspectives.

Theological Reflection

Christian theological reflection is needed to reflect upon the discovery of the Highland Settlements as a new origin story of the ancient Hebrew people. As discussed previously, this information has been discovered and interpreted by biblical scholars for decades, but Christian theologians and churches have not reflected upon this material theologically. What does the Highland Settlements story mean for the church? How can this story shape Christian identity?

Christian identity has been shaped, in part, through the appropriation of the Israelite conquest narrative. European Christian colonists saw North America as the New Promised Land and its indigenous people as "Canaanites," justifying the genocide of many Native American peoples.[1] It stands to reason, then, that the discovery of a new story of Hebrew origins can reshape Christian identity to reckon with our past and pursue a new future.

By theological reflection, I do not mean speculating on what

---

[1] Warrior explains how many Europeans viewed Native American people as Canaanites in Robert Warrior, "Canaanites, Cowboys, and Indians," *Christianity & Crisis* 49, no. 12 (September 11, 1989).

Iron Age theology the Highland Settlers might have believed. Instead, we must reflect on how the Highland Settlements story can speak with theological meaning for our present. How might Christian identity and imagination be constructed differently with the discovery of a new Hebrew origin story? What is God calling us to do or be today through the Highland Settlements story?

Theological reflection can enable glimpses beyond the status quo and can stimulate imagination, insight, and next steps for communities.[2] Theological reflection can also lead to repentance or *metanoia*, the Greek word for change of mind, which can lead to shifts in consciousness, self-understanding, and collective action toward embodying "empowering alternatives."[3] To change one's mind means to do and be differently, to turn around and walk away from sin. Such change may also mean walking away from certain theologies.

Churches are responsible for dealing with theological legacies that have empowered Christian colonialism; churches are also responsible for admitting to and seeking to make right the deep wrongs of Christian colonialization and genocide around the globe.[4] Theological reflection can be a step toward responsibly dealing with this past and generating new imagination for the future.

A first step toward repentance and reconciliation is to

---

[2]Stephen Lewis, Matthew Wesley Williams, and Dori Grinenko Baker, *Another Way: Living and Leading Change on Purpose* (St. Louis: Chalice, 2020), 109.

[3]Lewis, Williams, and Baker, *Another Way*, 112.

[4]Joyce Hope Scott, "POV: It's Time for Reparations and Transitional Justice for African Americans," *BU Today*, September 16, 2020. This article specifically looks at restorative justice for African American enslavement, but similar truths apply to considering the church's role not only in human enslavement but also other colonial atrocities.

acknowledge harm. Now more than ever, we need to look clearly at the violent realities of America's past and colonial Christianity's role in supporting a religious imagination that justified violence through violent images of God. To be sure, many pastors theologically reflect upon the conquest narrative and preach against it with historical-critical and challenging sermons, especially when conquest texts are scheduled as a lectionary text. I have personally heard several well-done sermons on the topic of conquest. But is critical preaching against these texts enough to deal responsibly with the legacies of violence and conquest of the church? From a restorative justice standpoint, sermons, while helpful, are not enough. More must be done. Furthermore, theological reflection must be a communal endeavor and not only the responsibility of the clergy. Communal theological reflection is needed upon the Hebrew Highland Settlements, the conquest narrative, the Christian colonial past, and the future of Christian practice.

Part of repentance is moving forward in a new way. Recentering the Highland Settlements as a liberating counterhistory of origins is one substantive way of moving forward differently. Much more will need to be done, but recentering the Highland Settlements in theological reflection and ecclesial practice can be a start.[5] Incorporating the Highland Settlements story into the life of the church through its worshiping life—its liturgical practices—can be a powerful and persistent way to theologically reflect on and practice new Christian identities.

---

[5] I use the word recenter to indicate that at some point in Hebrew history the Highland Settlements story was likely central to the historical tradition, before obfuscated by other histories.

Liturgical Innovations

Many churches already possess a system for incorporating new material into its communal life. Churches are liturgically and ritually focused communities that often communicate with their communities through symbols and metaphors. The symbols used in rituals communicate meaning in subtle ways; the practitioners who participate in the acting out of those symbols imbibe the meaning behind them gradually, eventually coming to accept what those symbols communicate not so much by direct intellectual assent but by living into the truth communicated.[6] By developing new scripts for thinking and being and incorporating them into the ritual and liturgical praxis, churches can counter or replace previous harmful models. Generating new symbols and altering ritual and liturgy do, in essence, what corporate rebranding practices do: they can organically and holistically alter our ways of thinking and being. To communicate new meaning or a shift in meaning, those same patterns of symbolic discourse must be utilized such that the worshipers participating in that discourse in the context of ritual will come to affirm the convictions latent in the symbols without facing a jarring disconnect or being overwhelmed by information.

The Highland Settlements story can be incorporated into existing liturgies. Considering certain liturgical practices specifically, I suggest innovations in weekly liturgy and also propose an entirely new liturgical season, called The Season of Origins. As will be discussed in detail, Origins is a yearly

---

[6]For discussion of ritual use of symbolic communication, see Bernard Cooke and Gary Macy, *Christian Symbol and Ritual* (New York: Oxford University Press, 2005).

practice designed to incorporate education and theological reflection on the Highland Settlements and related topics. Origins is designed to invite the Highland Settlements and other liberative origin stories into the life of the church. It is also meant to challenge and assist churches in dealing with legacies of violence in their own history and Christian history broadly. Lastly, it can facilitate reimagining ways that church can become more just and holistic to meet the many challenges of the day.

Weekly Liturgy

One possibility for recentering the Highland Settlements in ecclesial practice is to integrate the settlements story into weekly liturgical services. As briefly discussed above, the symbolic Highland Settlements exodus story in chapter 4 can become part of a weekly liturgical service. A liturgical reading of the Highland Settlements Exodus narration can serve as both a counterhistorical and reorienting liturgical moment. As a counterhistory it shows that the origin of the Hebrew people in Canaan does not begin with violence and genocide. Rather, it emphasizes that an innovative, communitas movement lies at the origins of the biblical traditions. People literally left empire to build new, more just communities. Just as the Lord's Prayer or the Nicene Creed are recited weekly in some churches, so, too, could the symbolic Highland Settlements exodus story become a regularly experienced text.

A liturgical reading can coincide with a time of meditation and confession. During this meditative time, the church is reminded that at the roots of the Hebrew tradition is the building of new communities in response to injustice, empire, and climate change. Next, a confessional moment can ask people to reflect upon the ways that they benefit from or are complicit with empire. Finally, people can be asked to consider the ways that they are working to subvert unjust practices and structures or build more just communities in their own contexts as a symbolic participation in the Highland Settlements exodus story. Such a liturgical moment brings the settlements story into the life of the church in a weekly ritualized way, enabling people to reflect on the story and to create space for the story to shape imagination. Liturgically reading the story can be an important starting point and foundation for even larger liturgical innovations.

The Season of Origins

For the settlements to become a new image that can prompt radical imagination in the church and beyond, even more will need to be done than a weekly liturgical reading, book study, or sermon series. Though such practices are necessary starting points, they are not enough. Radical imagination needs sustained, repetitive, and memorable praxis to take root. I propose the development and implementation of a brand-new liturgical season, what I am naming The Season of Origins (Origins). Origins is designed to integrate the Highland Settlements story more fully into the Christian tradition and enable the story to take root, sprout radical imagination, and reshape people in its path.[7]

Launching a new liturgical season is, no doubt, a large undertaking, but it matches the profundity of the discovery of the Highland Settlements and the change required of the

---

[7]The idea to develop a new liturgical season came about in part through conversation with Mary Elizabeth Moore, to whom I am grateful for her mentorship and insights over the years.

current moment. Some might think it is too radical or risky to invent and launch a new liturgical season, yet the liturgical seasons themselves are products of changing Christian traditions that incorporated the old with the new. Early Christian worship patterns followed a diverse variety of cycles, with the seven-day week, "which was taken over from Judaism by the first Christians but came to be centered on 'the Lord's day' rather than the Sabbath," as the fundamental rhythm of life.[8] For hundreds of years, Christians worshiped in overlapping cycles that observed Easter or Pascha, Lent, Holy Week, Christmas and Epiphany, and saints' days.[9] The liturgical year emerged as a cohesive concept "from the late sixteenth century onwards," note Paul Bradshaw and Maxwell Johnson.[10] Incorporating the Highland Settlements story through a new liturgical Season of Origins is an opportunity for the church today to recognize and celebrate the diversity of its own origins, joining traditional cycles in a "kaleidoscope of changing feasts, fasts, and seasons" that mark the worshiping life of our communities.[11]

Radical praxis is needed to subvert the hegemonic status quo and to spark new imagination for the future. If you are worried about making such a change, perhaps reflect on the current circumstances: can we continue with the present trajectory? Patriarchal, white-supremacist, and imperialistic regimes have hundreds, if not thousands, of years of inertia careening them forward and threatening irreparable collapse for all. To interrupt this force, to alter course, we need radical change.

---

[8]Paul F. Bradshaw and Maxwell E. Johnson, *The Origins of Feasts, Fasts, and Seasons in Early Christianity* (Collegeville, MN: Liturgical Press, 2016), xiii.

[9]Bradshaw and Johnson, *Origins*, xiii–xvi.

[10]Bradshaw and Johnson, *Origins*, xiii.

[11]Bradshaw and Johnson, *Origins*, xvi.

Practicing Origins

The Season of Origins creates a yearly opportunity to focus on the work of undoing conquest, to facilitate healing the wounds of the past, to imagine the change we need for the challenges of the present moment, and to integrate the Highland Settlements story into the Christian tradition. Several key principles can guide the season, its rituals, and its practices: learn and reflect on the Highland Settlements, gain and enhance biblical literacy, understand the impact of history on the present, engage both problematic and liberative histories, and imagine more just futures and practices. These principles are derived from the topics and practices that have been discussed throughout this book. For communities that are unable or unwilling to implement a new liturgical season, the many practices that follow may be implemented as individual practices throughout the year.

The Liturgical Calendar

The current liturgical calendar in most Western Christian ecumenical traditions include these key seasons: Advent, Christmas, Ordinary Time after Epiphany, Lent, Easter, and Ordinary Time after Pentecost.[12] The Ordinary Time after Pentecost is over six months long, encompassing the second half of the liturgical year. Origins can be situated here. I propose that Origins takes place during four weeks in October, beginning on the Sunday that directly precedes Indigenous Peoples' Day in the United States. This will typically be the second Sunday of the month as Indigenous Peoples' Day falls

---

[12]Hoyt Hickman, *New Handbook of the Christian Year: Based on the Revised Common Lectionary* (Nashville: Abingdon, 2010), 31.

on the second Monday in October. Indigenous Peoples' Day is a countercelebration of the US federal holiday Columbus Day and is marked as a day of celebration of and solidarity with Indigenous Peoples.[13] There is a resonant synergy between Origins and Indigenous Peoples' Day as Origins emphasizes the importance of reparation, reconciliation, and healing for the many atrocities perpetrated against Indigenous Peoples by European Christian settlers. Origins can amplify Indigenous Peoples' Day within churches.

Like Advent, Origins is a four-week-long season. By launching Origins during October, churches can use September to welcome congregants back after the summer months (in the northern hemisphere), establishing new rhythms before launching into a liturgical season. The first week in October is World Communion Sunday, so launching Origins during the second week can build on World Communion for those churches that celebrate it. Furthermore, since September is typically a busy back-to-school month and education is on our minds, October is a good time to invite people into a period of study and learning, which is a hallmark of the Origins season.

By ending Origins on the last Sunday in October or the first Sunday in November, it will be close to All Saints' Day, which is a day of remembrance that can also remind us to recall our origins and the ancestors who have come before us. Instituting Origins prior to Advent orients the season chronologically before the birth of Christ, which makes it a temporal reminder that the roots of Christianity are found within the Hebrew tradition. Advent is full of readings from the prophets of the

---

[13]Many states and municipalities in the United States officially celebrate Indigenous Peoples' Day, and President Joe Biden formally commemorated it through a presidential proclamation in 2021. However, it has not yet become a federal US holiday.

Hebrew Bible and begins each new Christian liturgical year. Seasons of Origins would return the worshiping community to the roots of these prophetic voices in a recapitulation near the end of the liturgical year. The Highland Settlements story will be the overarching historical event guiding the season, just as the birth of Christ orients Christmas and the passion of Christ orients Easter.

Origins marks a particular time of year as the time to do healing work on behalf of our past, imagining new futures in turn, and bringing to the fore the intersecting nature of the past, present, and future. Autumn in the northern hemisphere evokes contrary feelings of both nostalgia and new beginnings. It is simultaneously a time of homecoming—a return to our roots and reflection on our past—while also a back-to-school time filled with all the eagerness and newness that comes with new beginnings. It is a time of reflection on, celebration of, and harvest from the abundance of our labors. Such feelings mimic the overarching principles of Origins. Origins is a return home to the origins of the Hebrew tradition and a chance to reshape the Christian tradition into the future. The intertwining tension between past and present is tangible in the crisp autumn air, presenting a perfect time in which to locate the Season of Origins.

Just as Advent is oriented on different weekly themes (hope, peace, joy, and love), I suggest four themes to accompany the four weeks of Origins: Invite, Name, Repair, and Imagine. These themes orient each week of Origins in a progressive cycle: *invite* new histories and texts; *name* the role of Christian atrocities, past and present; *repair* harm; *imagine* new futures.[14] These are provoking themes to be sure, but Origins

---

[14]These four themes echo the basic principles of restorative justice (Repair, Acknowledge, Transformation). Restorative justice theories and practices can

is meant to challenge. One of the weekly themes can also become the overarching focus of each year, in a four-year cycle. The themes scaffold Origins as a seasonal healing process that involves repentance and reconciliation of past harms found throughout the Christian and ecclesiastical traditions. Repentance and reconciliation are key theological aspects of Origins. We cannot move forward until we do the difficult work of repentance. Much is needed to heal.

Churches, depending upon their demographic makeup, will tailor the Season of Origins toward their specific context. Predominantly white churches may focus on white supremacy and the churches' role in white settler colonialism, the genocide of Native Americans, and the capture and enslavement of African peoples. In turn, they could explore liberation theologies and the ways the white churches took part in abolitionist movements, resisted white supremacy, genocide, and slavery. Black churches or churches that predominantly comprise BIPOC people may orient the Season of Origins as a time to name grief, acknowledge the leaders of the past who helped to resist white supremacist atrocities, as well as lifting up liberative theologies of Christianity. These are just a few examples that illustrate how Origins can be tailored to meet the unique needs of churches. Though expressed differently, the Season of Origins unifies by marking a time of year where communal focus turns toward the Highland Settlements, healing the past, and imagining new futures.

Invite

The first week of Origins creates an opportunity to invite broader education and reflection on the influence that origin

---

certainly be useful resources for planning practices or events during Origins.

stories have in shaping communities. This week can be a time to center the Highland Settlements and to host a new ritual based around the story. It is also a time to discuss the importance of history and its role in shaping social imagination and social change. Invite is a time also meant to introduce other newly discovered texts and liberative biblical interpretations into the community. For example, gospel narratives could be introduced that are not included in the New Testament, like the Nag Hammadi text known as the *Gospel of Mary Magdalene*. Adult education or book studies could read womanist, feminist, and other liberation theologies that provide alternative interpretations of the biblical stories and the history of Christianity and the church. *Sisters in the Wilderness, The Christian Imagination, Saving Paradise, Violence to Eternity*, and *In Memory of Her* are all fitting texts for this season.[15] Invite can also be time for churches to reflect on the origins of their own congregation or their town, or the history of First Peoples or Native Americans in their region.

Name

Name is a week to invite churches to reflect upon and name their own origins, which includes taking responsibility for injustices like racial injustice and genocide. During this time, churches can reflect on themes of empire: defining and describ-

---

[15]Delores S. Williams, *Sisters in the Wilderness: The Challenge of Womanist God-Talk* (Maryknoll, NY: Orbis, 1993); Willie James Jennings, *The Christian Imagination: Theology and the Origins of Race* (New Haven, CT: Yale University Press, 2010); Rita Nakashima Brock and Rebecca Ann Parker, *Saving Paradise: How Christianity Traded Love of This World for Crucifixion and Empire* (Boston: Beacon Press, 2008); Grace M. Jantzen, *Violence to Eternity*, ed. Jeremy Carrette and Morny Joy (London: Routledge, 2009); Elisabeth Schüssler Fiorenza, *In Memory of Her: A Feminist Theological Reconstruction of Christian Origins*, 10th ann. ed. (New York: Crossroad, 1994).

ing the forms of empire and examining how the church both supports and subverts its practices. The week can be a time for reflecting on the origin of the Christian church in relation and resistance to the Roman Empire. Reflecting on broader themes of empire can lead to considering the origins of individual churches and denominations, including the ways they have resisted or supported oppression, imperialism, and even genocide. For example, where relevant, church communities could reflect on their connections with the oppression and genocide of Native Americans in the region. They could reflect on their history of condoning the enslavement of African Americans and how they perpetuate racial injustice today. In turn, it is also the week to name liberative and justice-seeking Christian traditions, including how churches worked toward abolition and civil rights. Churches could reflect on European reform movements in the sixteenth and seventeenth centuries that were based on resistance to oppression by the church itself or by a state church against others. These are just a few examples of topics that can be explored from a framework of accountability for injustice and the desire for reconciliation and a healing of the past. Name could include a ritual of lament and confession for the atrocities that have been done in the name of the church.

Repair

After naming the patterns of injustice, Repair turns focus to the work that is needed to make the church and society more just. Repair is a time to imagine how the church can seek to address the harms caused to and to reconcile with others. It can also be a time to introduce new justice-seeking practices and projects. Each church would approach this week differently depending upon its own history in relation to colonialism, racism, sexism, homophobia, or transphobia. Restorative justice models and practices will be an important resource to guide churches through reparative processes. There is need for institutional leadership in the United States to facilitate restorative justice work. Unlike a nation like South Africa, which conducted the South African Truth and Reconciliation Commission as one step toward reparative justice, the United States has not undertaken any similar measure to deal with the violence of the past. Nor has the church. Repair centers this important and necessary work. The church can step into this vacuum and lead the way in supporting and implementing reparations programs or other justice-seeking work. While many churches already do social justice work, Repair can be an annual liturgical time dedicated to the process of healing deep historical wounds as a necessary part of imagining and building a better future.

Imagine

Imagine is a week to tell the settlements story again, this time celebrating themes like bravery, for the settlers daring to start something new; ingenuity, for leveraging new technologies to build viable communities in rugged lands during a climate change; and communitas, for creating a social organization that contrasted with empire. It is also a time of celebrating the miraculous: a large, oppressive empire collapsed; a communitas movement made up of diverse peoples surviving just out of reach of empire; and the recent archaeological discovery of these settlements over three thousand years later. All of this marks the origins of the Hebrew people and biblical traditions. The Highland Settlements are truly an astonishing, even miraculous discovery.

The womanist theme of "making a way out of no way"

speaks to God in partnership with humans to create new opportunities of survival, encapsulating the spirit of Imagine.[16] Making a way out of no way, in womanist theology and African American heritage, emphasizes that human agency, ingenuity, and action are needed to bring the miraculous into the world. Imagine is a time to uplift and celebrate the lives of historical activists like Harriet Tubman, Fredrick Douglass, Ida B. Wells, Abraham Lincoln, Sojourner Truth, Howard Thurman, Martin Luther King Jr., and Rachel Carson, to name only a few who have carried the torch of justice and freedom for all peoples and the environment, carving ways out of no way. We celebrate the good of the past to bolster our own spirits and imaginations as we embark on change projects to help bring about a better world.

The conclusion of Imagine and of the yearly season is a time to invite congregations to reimagine ways that they can use their own resources, ingenuity, and creativity to create a better world or embark upon their own communitas movement. How can the church help create a more just way of life where all people can flourish? How can we reimagine church through inspiration from the Highland Settlements?

As the description of the four weeks of Origins illustrates, the monthlong season is a communal ritual container that invites the Highland Settlements story and other liberative origin stories into the life of the church. It is also a time to focus on issues such as histories of violence and oppression, racial injustice, and others to make sure they are revisited yearly. Like

---

[16]Coleman, *Making a Way out of No Way: A Womanist Theology* (Minneapolis: Fortress Press, 2008), 33. Monica Coleman traces the concept "making a way out of no way" in womanist theology through the works of Jacquelyn Grant, Kelly Brown Douglas, Delores S. Williams, JoAnne Marie Terrell, and Karen Baker Fletcher. She shows that a survival thread runs through all of these womanist works.

peeling an onion, healing work is often multilayered. Time is often needed to process grief in order to move to another level of awareness and healing. Such work cannot be rushed. Origins ensures that this healing and integrative work does not fall to the wayside but is embedded into the rhythms of the church year. The season provides opportunity for different churches to come together, deal with these themes, seek ways to heal, and imagine new futures.

Conclusion

The Highland Settlements speak today. They challenge the biblical story of conquest and the legacies of violence justified by it. They ask us to look anew at the Bible and how we understand its stories and grant authority to its words. They call us to reimagine community in the face of empire and climate change. As a newly discovered origin story, at the root of the biblical traditions, the Highland Settlements can prompt reimagination of the mission and identity of church. In turn, they can prompt churches to reimagine how to leverage existing resources to embody the gospel in more just and holistic ways.

Deep resonances exist with current cultural contexts in the United States and those in Canaan at the end of the Bronze Age—crushing debt, climate change, political instability, and extreme socioeconomic disparity between the elite classes and the poor. The Highland Settlers responded to these ecological and social problems by breaking new ground and building new communities. With the many challenges facing our world, and many people grappling with the atrocities of history, now is the time to invite the Highland Settlements to shape us—to make new meaning out of the past. The foundational community-building practice of the Highland Settlers in the face of extreme social and ecological conditions can provide an orienting vision for churches today that seek guidance in their practice from the historical tradition. The Highland Settlements can help undo the power of conquest in the Christian imagination and inspire new vision for communities right now.

Epilogue

The Highland Settlers faced climate change, extreme economic injustice, enslavement, and civilization collapse. Remarkably, we find ourselves in a similar cultural and ecological situation. Despite temporal and technological differences, we too inhabit unjust societal systems nested within unstable political environments, and we are faced with unprecedented ecological crises from superstorms to fires, floods, and droughts. We are at the edge of collapse.[1] Collapse need not be the end. Instead, collapse must be a new beginning.

Faced with similar conditions, the ancestors of the Israelites built new communities as a necessary survival response to their world. They leveraged the resources before them to build a new way of life together. How they lived illustrates the ingenuity of oppressed peoples seeking to carve out more just ways of life across the ages. The Highland Settlers left a lasting impact that has reverberated throughout the millennia through the prophetic biblical traditions. Now, their story is finally being told, and it can help us to understand the origins of our biblical faith tradi-

---

[1]Margaret Wheatley argues that Western civilization is at the end of its life cycle and follows the typical pattern of civilization collapse every 250 years or ten generations. She argues that leadership during a time of collapse is about "making a profound difference locally, in the lives of people in their communities and organizations." Margaret Wheatley, *Who Do We Choose to Be? Facing Reality, Claiming Leadership, Restoring Sanity* (Oakland: Berrett-Koehler, 2017), 48.

tions more fully. Given that origin stories shape identity, how can the Highland Settlements story reshape Christian identity, which looks to Israelite origins as a precursor to its own?

I studied the Highland Settlements story as a practical theologian for nearly a decade, reflecting upon theological questions: How is God speaking through the discovery of the Highland Settlements? What might God be calling the church to do or be through the discovery of the Highland Settlements? In response to these questions, I hear God calling us to innovation, to communitas, to the forming of holistic, pluralistic communities that seek to subvert the oppressive status quo by modeling more just community-building on the edges of empire, leveraging the technology and resources that are available to create a different way of life. We can transform ourselves to transform the world.[2]

What if churches, inspired by the historical image of the Highland Settlements, decided that their mission was to develop holistic, innovative communities, small "islands of sanity," or communities of care designed to be more sustainable and communal than individualistic ways of life?[3] What if the mission of church was to develop more just ways of life in partnership with the Divine in the face of climate change and economic, racial, and gender injustices? That is, what if building holistic communities became the heart of how we interpret the Gospel and the structure and practice of church?

Through the story of the Highland Settlers, God is calling us to pick up our tools and build anew. What do you hear?

---

[2]Adrienne M. Brown, *Emergent Strategy* (Chico, CA: AK Press, 2017), 64.

[3]Wheatley argues that creating what she calls "islands of sanity" is a way to move forward despite collapse. For her, islands of sanity are defined as "places of possibility and sanctuary where the destructive dynamics of collapse are at bay." Wheatley, *Who Do We Choose to Be?*, 49.

Appendix

Resources for Religious Education,
Sermons, Biblical Literacy,
and Theological Reflection in Dialogue
with the Highland Settlements

Religious Education and Sermon Topics

Religious education classes, book studies, sermon series, or guest speakers are educational media that can be used to introduce the Highland Settlements to faith communities. Most people are unaware of Highland Settlements research outside of academic theology, so educational activities can be an important way to introduce people to the discovery. Possible topics for religious education classes or sermons could be "Communal Origins: Introducing the Highland Settlements," "Undoing Conquest: Understanding the Bible and Conquest," and "The Importance of History for Social Justice." These are just samples of topics that could be further developed from the content discussed in *Undoing Conquest*. Such topics could be developed for theological school courses, topics of study, or lectures.

Undoing Conquest is designed to introduce people to the Highland Settlements and could be read and discussed over several weeks in a small-group book study. If people would like even more information on the settlements discovery, the book *Who Were the Ancient Israelites and Where Did They Come From?*, written by archaeologist William Dever, provides an in-depth and accessible discussion of the intricate details of the archaeological evidence.[1] Norman Gottwald's classic tome *The Tribes of Yahweh* first interpreted the Highland Settlements research from a sociological and social justice perspective and is a book for folks who have even further interest in the subject. Gottwald's book has inspired base communities in Latin America and political prisoners from South Korea to South Africa.

The Importance of History

Learning more about the Highland Settlements creates an opportunity to study the importance of history and how it affects the present. Throughout this book, I discuss the importance of history in shaping individuals, communities, and cultures. History is embodied in the present. The Highland Settlements discovery invites a dialogue about how histories function to shape both individual and communal identity; the entanglement of history and power, that is, how history can be shaped to support domination, and how counterhistories can subvert dominant histories and power; and the necessity to deal with violent histories *and* the violence in our own histories, to seek justice in the present and create better futures. The Highland Settlements can be a catalyst to delve into these historical topics alongside learning more about the origins

---

[1]William G. Dever, *Who Were the Ancient Israelites and Where Did They Come From?* (Grand Rapids: Eerdmans Publishing, 2006).

of the Israelite people, the production of the biblical texts, and how Israelite history is shaped in certain ways through the biblical texts. Integrating the Highland Settlements into faith communities creates an opening to deal with topics of history more broadly and highlights the necessity of dealing with histories of violence, particularly within Christianity.

Churches can lead historical healing work by exploring their local history from a restorative justice model. Restorative justice models help communities openly deal with past harm.[2] Questions like the following can be explored: Are there events or issues from the past that need to be acknowledged, repaired, and transformed? On what land is the church built? How did the church come to inhabit this place? Was the church built as part of white settler colonialism? What First Nations people were caretakers of this land before they were forcibly removed? Land acknowledgments can be a basic first step for bringing to consciousness the genocide and cultural erasure at the foundations of the society we inhabit. Other historical lines of questions can explore whether a faith community has historically supported social justice movements. For example, did the community support the abolitionist movements or the civil rights movements? How has the community historically treated women, BIPOC, and LGBTQ+ peoples? These same questions can be asked at a wider denominational level or explored from a geographic regional perspective.

Communities need not wade into this work alone. Practical help is out there. The book *Healing Haunted Histories: A Settler Discipleship of Decolonization* is a useful tool for

---

[2]For a comprehensive resource on restorative justice models, see Howard Zehr et al., eds., *The Big Book of Restorative Justice: Four Classic Justice & Peacebuilding Books in One Volume*, revised and updated (New York: Good Books, 2015).

guiding necessary decolonizing and reparative historical work.[3] It explores European settlement of North America through lenses of trauma, unawareness, and complicity while also providing a practical workbook for guiding decolonizing practices. The book "tackles the oldest and deepest injustices on this continent" and seeks "to build capacity for the work of decolonization as a commitment to heal those wounds."[4] Books like *Undoing Conquest* and *Healing Haunted Histories* pair well for inviting communities into this healing work.

In July 2022, Pope Francis explicitly acknowledged the past harms of the Catholic Church upon Indigenous communities in Canada during a Canadian papal visit intended to help communities heal from atrocities the church had committed. The papal tour, titled "Walking Together, Healing and Reconciliation: An Historic Journey," provided an opportunity for Pope Francis "to listen and dialogue with Indigenous Peoples, to express his heartfelt closeness and to address the impact of colonization and the participation of the Catholic Church in the operation of residential schools throughout Canada."[5] The official aim of the visit was for the Catholic Church "to take genuine and meaningful steps to journey with Indigenous Peoples of this land on the lengthy path to healing and reconciliation."[6] While the trip was described by some Indigenous Canadians as being full of tension, it was nevertheless significant for the act of a public apology by the pope for the brutal harms

---

[3] Elaine Enns and Ched Myers, *Healing Haunted Histories: A Settler Discipleship of Decolonization*, Center and Library for the Bible and Social Justice (Eugene, OR: Cascade, 2021).

[4] Enns and Myers, *Healing Haunted Histories,* xxii.

[5] "Pope Francis in Canada—Walking Together," Pope Francis in Canada website, 2022.

[6] "Pope Francis in Canada—Walking Together."

inflicted by the Catholic boarding schools.[7] The pope's visit
sparked a call for the Catholic Church to officially rescind the
Doctrine of Discovery that justified Western colonialism of
the Americas.[8] The visit and the Indigenous Peoples' response
to the tour illustrate how important and relevant this type of
historical work remains—and how much still remains undone.

OWHN: Our Whole History Now

The United States will never heal from its past if history is
told in whitewashed ways. The same is true for the church. If
both America and the church wish to live into their respective
democratic and gospel ideals, then the past must be addressed
directly. Despite the need for nuanced historical teaching,
many states and school boards are currently placing bans on
teaching marginalized, critical histories in public schools. This
politically reactive context creates an opening for churches to
lead the way in teaching accurate and nuanced American history. Because US history is deeply intertwined with Christian
imagination and the church, US history need not only be the
purview of public education. If the church wishes to repent
and reconcile the sins of the past, then dealing with history is
a necessary step. As cultural and political flames are stoked,
the church can lead conversation on the importance of understanding marginalized histories.

Here, I am imagining the development of a curriculum
for US history like the Our Whole Lives: Lifespan Sexuality
Education for Youth (OWL) curriculum. OWL was developed
by the Unitarian Universalist Association (UUA) and the

[7]Stephanie Taylor, "Papal Apology Sparks Calls to Renounce 500-Year-Old Doctrine of Discovery," Global News, July 30, 2022.

[8]Taylor, "Papal Apology Sparks Calls to Renounce 500-Year-Old Doctrine of Discovery."

United Church of Christ (UCC) and is "a comprehensive, lifespan sexuality education curricula" designed to fill the need of "accurate, developmentally appropriate" sex education for youth, since most public schools do not offer such teaching.[9] OWL is designed to be utilized in both secular and faith-based contexts. Similarly, churches could offer comprehensive US history in places where accurate, multicultural historical education is not offered in schools. Historical curricula could be developed for adults and youth that mirrors the OWL program in design, with comprehensive US history content. The curriculum could be called Our Whole History Now, or OWHN, a homonym to the word "own"—it is time to own our whole history now as a church and a nation. By developing a historical curriculum like OWHN, churches can provide comprehensive historical education in places where local or state governments have banned critical history in schools. Churches can lead the way in doing this necessary historical healing work.

Enhancing Biblical Literacy

Undoing Conquest shows how the Highland Settlements archaeological evidence of Hebrew origins challenges the biblical story of conquest. The challenge raises questions about the Bible and creates an opportunity for biblical study. Here, I do not mean a Bible study of interpreting specific texts, but an introduction to wider biblical literacy—that is, knowing more about the Bible, its content, and how it was produced. If the Hebrew people emerged in Canaan through a peaceful, indigenous settlement process, why does the biblical con-

---

[9]"Our Whole Lives: Lifespan Sexuality Education," Unitarian Universalist Association, 2023.

quest story depict the Israelites as violent and non-Canaanite outsiders? Biblical scholarship offers answers to the question by providing a window into the social and political context of the writers of the conquest narrative. As such, introducing the Highland Settlements invites the opportunity to examine historical- and source-critical theories of who wrote the Bible, as well as broader conversation about the Hebrew Bible, understanding major textual sources, and theories on authorship and editorial compilation.

Whether you hold the Bible as sacred Scripture or not, the Bible is an important culture-shaping artifact in many societies. The Bible "encodes Western culture's central myth of collective identity," Regina Schwartz argues.[10] US culture wars and racial, gender, sexuality, and economic injustice are often supported by certain oppressive interpretations of biblical texts. Therefore, a more fulsome understanding of the Bible is important even for people who do not consider the Bible to be a sacred text. Social justice work can only be served by a deeper understanding of the roots of the cultural legacies we are embedded within, like the Bible. These roots are what designers, practical theologians, and sociologists call a "thick description," or a nuanced understanding of what is going on below the surface of a community or culture. Biblical literacy can be helpful for anyone or any community that seeks to create more just policies and institutions and is passionate about altering inherited lineages of violence. In particular, it is important to understand the parts of the Bible, like the conquest narrative, that have shaped social imagination in harmful and violent ways.

Greater biblical literacy can demystify the sociopolitical

---

[10]Regina M. Schwartz, *The Curse of Cain: The Violent Legacy of Monotheism* (Chicago: University of Chicago Press, 1997), 6.

contexts that led to the writing of certain biblical texts like the Deuteronomistic History and the conquest narrative. Biblical literacy can also help to combat fundamentalist, literal interpretations of the Bible that often support oppressive theologies and practices. Biblicist interpretations of biblical texts tend to dominate what gets labeled as "Christian perspectives" in the public sphere. Greater understanding of the Bible can enhance progressive Christian counterinterpretations to harmful fundamentalist biblicist perspectives. Such learning can also enhance spiritual and devotional connection to the Bible by demystifying it and grounding it within history. For myself, studying biblical scholarship has given me much greater appreciation of the Bible in my own spiritual life.

The Documentary Hypothesis and Overview of Early Biblical Sources

Before the advent of biblical scholarship, a popular theory existed that Moses wrote the Pentateuch (the first five books of the Bible: Genesis, Exodus, Leviticus, Numbers, and Deuteronomy). However, some noticed that there were redundancies in the Pentateuch, and since Deuteronomy reports Moses's death, it would have been impossible for him to write all five books. Recognizing and paying attention to these details led to nearly three centuries of biblical scholarship, a broad discourse that provides rich details on the literary, historical, and contextual details surrounding the biblical texts. In particular, the writing and development of the Pentateuch and former prophets has been an important topic in biblical scholarship.[11]

---

[11]As David Carr explains, "Scholars have seen evidence for this for centuries, starting with a German pastor, Henning Bernard Witter. Three hundred years ago, in 1711, he noticed ways that the story of creation in Genesis 1 both doubled and diverged from the story of creation in Genesis 2." David M. Carr,

The Pentateuchal books are now commonly thought to be made up of a combination of several different sources that have been braided or edited together to form the different books as they now exist in the Bible. The theory of the braided formation of these books is called the "documentary hypothesis," positing that there are four primary sources—or documents—found within the Pentateuch and the former prophets known as the Yahwist (J), Elohist (E), Deuteronomist (D), and Priestly (P) sources. This brief description of the documentary hypothesis illustrates that the early books of the Bible are a complex library of sources that span centuries and authors.

The Yahwist source, or J, gets its name because it uses the name Yahweh for God.[12] Likewise, the Elohist, or E, source uses Elohim for God. Both J and E are typically considered older sources, possibly dating from around the ninth century BCE.[13] The Deuteronomist, or D, source contains the Deuteronomistic History (DH), and spans the books of Deuteronomy, Joshua, Judges, Samuel, and Kings. An early edition of D was likely written during the reign of King Hezekiah with a major revision with key additions (like the book of Joshua) composed during the reign of King Josiah in Judah, as well as additional updates and redactions to the DH done during the Babylonian exile.[14] Lastly, the Priestly, or P, source is a

"The Formation of the Hebrew Bible," in *The Wiley Blackwell Companion to Ancient Israel*, ed. Susan Niditch (Malden, MA: Wiley Blackwell, 2016), 107.

[12]Even though it is the Yahwist source, the letter J symbolizes the name "Jehovah," which is the term for Yahweh used in the German language, from which the first Yahwist research came from.

[13]Not all agree with an early dating of J. John Van Seters argues that J was a source written in the exile as a prologue to the Deuteronomistic History. See John Van Seters, *The Yahwist: A Historian of Israelite Origins* (Winona Lake, IN: Eisenbrauns, 2013).

[14]The following make an argument for a major edition of the Deuteronomistic History as being produced during the Josianic era: Frank Moore Cross,

narrative layer produced during or closely after the Babylonian exile, weaving together all of these other sources into a cohesive set of texts. P also added new stories when needed, redacted narratives, and smoothed over obvious narrative seams or disjunctures between the different sources in order to make a somewhat unified and cohesive narrative.

While the basic contours of the documentary hypothesis have been prominent for nearly a century, there are updates and differences in perspectives among scholars. For example, some doubt the existence of a long Yahwistic or Elohist source, suggesting that there may have existed independent Jacob, Moses, and Abraham stories that were joined together by priestly scribes.[15] Some think that the J source was not an early source but was written later, during the Babylonian exile, as a prologue to the Deuteronomistic History. Despite some disagreement on the details of the documentary hypothesis, there is nearly a consensus that the Priestly and Deuteronomistic sources existed and that "the Pentateuch was formed over time through a combination of joining, conflation, redaction, and counterwriting."[16] The formation of the Bible was a long and complex process.

Canaanite Myth and Hebrew Epic (Cambridge, MA: Harvard University Press, 1973); Steven L. McKenzie, *The Trouble with Kings: The Composition of the Book of Kings in the Deuteronomistic History*, Supplements to Vetus Testamentum 42 (Leiden: E. J. Brill, 1991), 150; Richard D. Nelson, "Josiah in the Book of Joshua," *Journal of Biblical Literature* 100, no. 4 (December 1981): 531–40; Richard D. Nelson, *The Double Redaction of the Deuteronomistic History*, JSOTSup 18 (Sheffield: JSOT Press, Department of Biblical Studies, University of Sheffield, 1981); Thomas Römer, *The So-Called Deuteronomistic History: A Sociological, Historical, and Literary Introduction* (London: T&T Clark, 2005); Marvin Sweeney, *King Josiah of Judah: The Lost Messiah of Israel* (Oxford: Oxford University Press, 2001), 25.

[15]Carr, "The Formation of the Hebrew Bible," 113.

[16]Carr, "The Formation of the Hebrew Bible," 114.

Suggestions for Further Learning

Biblical scholars have produced excellent and accessible books geared toward introducing biblical scholarship to a nonspecialist audience. These books would be good texts for a book group. For example, the book *Who Wrote the Bible?* is written for nonacademic audiences and presents biblical scholarship about the sources of the Hebrew Bible in accessible ways.[17] The present book, *Undoing Conquest,* can be used as a primer for understanding both the Highland Settlements and the Deuteronomistic source of the Hebrew Bible. The book *A Short History of the New Testament* provides basic literacy of New Testament scholarship.[18] It introduces the contexts and contents of the New Testament texts while also discussing the influence of the New Testament in Western culture.

Churches with monetary resources could hire a local biblical scholar to teach a Bible 101 course over a few weeks. Such a course could be open to people outside the church as a public service to encourage biblical literacy in the broader community. Other more readily accessible educational options are free massive open online courses (MOOCs) that teach about the Bible. For example, during the writing of this book, two courses have been available for free on the web platforms Coursera and edX: *The Bible's Prehistory, Purpose, and Political Future* (Coursera, from Emory University); and *Christianity through Its Scriptures* (edX, from Harvard Divinity School).[19] These

---

[17]Richard Elliott Friedman, *Who Wrote the Bible?* (New York: Simon & Schuster, 2019).

[18]Halvor Moxnes, *A Short History of the New Testament*, I. B. Tauris Short Histories (London: Tauris, 2014). Thanks to Dr. Ryan Schellenberg for recommending this book.

[19]Jacob L. Wright, "The Bible's Prehistory, Purpose, and Political Future," Coursera, 2023; Karen L. King and Sarah Griffis, "Christianity through Its Scriptures," edX, 2023.

courses, taught by biblical scholars and theologians, provide a free opportunity for people to learn about the content and contexts of the biblical texts from experts. These are just a few ways that communities and individuals who are not enrolled in a seminary can access educational resources that provide the richness of knowledge about the Bible produced by the biblical scholars over the centuries.

Practicing Theological Reflection

Earlier, I discussed the importance of reflecting on how the Highland Settlements story speaks theologically for the present. Individuals can do such theological reflection alone, or it can be done together in a group. Churches or other communities may consider forming a theological reflection group to meet and engage in the reflective practice communally. I suggest creating a prayerful or meditative space and inviting your heart as well as your mind into the process. Be creative and open to the wisdom that will emerge from your practice.

To begin, start your theological reflection focused on the conquest narrative. The book of Joshua counters the Highland Settlements archaeological evidence in many ways, and theological insight can emerge within the contrast of the two stories. Because most people are more familiar with the book of Joshua than the Highland Settlements, theological reflection can be easier with something known. Also, theological reflection on the settlements story that comes from archaeological and biblical studies discourse might feel awkward at first. Starting with something more familiar will be helpful, and questions and reflective practice upon the Joshua text can then be mirrored with the Highland Settlements evidence.

Start by reading and reflecting on the conquest narrative in the book of Joshua (chs. 3–9). After prayerful or meditative reading, the following questions can help to guide theological reflection on the text. How do you imagine God in the conquest story? What is God calling people to do through the conquest story? What actions are justified by God in the conquest narrative? What kind of people does the conquest story imagine the people of God to be?

These questions may be difficult to answer, and the answers may be surprising, but they can help underscore how violent biblical texts can shape violent theological interpretations, actions, and images of God. Be aware how such effects may be heightened when discussing an origin story, which can serve in shaping the fundamental building blocks of religious identity.

Next, turn to the Highland Settlements evidence. Since there is not a biblical text that explicitly narrates the early settlements period, a place to start can be reading chapter 2 of this book again, perhaps in a prayerful or meditative state, and asking similar reflection questions.[20] How do you imagine God in the Highland Settlements story, or more specifically, how do you imagine God acting in the Highlands Settlements story? What is God calling people to do or be through the Highland Settlements story? What actions are justified by God in the Highland Settlements story? If origin stories contribute to the shaping of identity, how might we be shaped anew by the settlements story? What is the settlements story calling us to do?

Now that you have reflected on both the conquest narrative and the Highland Settlements story, you can reflect on

---

[20]Though the books of Judges and Exodus illustrate aspects of the settlements period, they do not constitute an explicit story of the early Iron Age I Highland Settlements time, like what is revealed through archaeological evidence.

the answers to your different questions together. How does your imagining of God differ between the two stories? Are there redeemable characteristics of God from your theological reflection on Joshua? If so, why? If not, why not? What responsibility does the church have in dealing with a text like Joshua?

Another relevant topic of reflection considers that the Highland Settlements were unknown until their discovery during the last one hundred years. How do we make meaning of the fact that the settlements history was once lost and is now found, literally unearthed? How do you imagine God in this process? Is God speaking something through this discovery? What might God be calling us to do through the discovery of the Highland Settlements? Where is God in the discovery of the Highland Settlements archaeological evidence?

By reflecting on these questions, new wisdom can emerge that can help to guide communities and churches into re-imagining their identity and practice. I answer these questions from my own theological reflection on these topics throughout *Undoing Conquest*. However, I challenge people to reflect for themselves and discover what wisdom emerges through them. While my theological imagination has perhaps influenced your reflections through this book, the Highland Settlements story encourages each of us to bring our own theological reflections to the proverbial campfire, sharing and learning together.

Additional resources can aid in this theological reflection practice. For example, the book *Joshua in 3-D: A Commentary on Biblical Conquest and Manifest Destiny,* by Daniel Hawk, can support nuanced theological reflection on the conquest narrative. *Joshua in 3-D* is a commentary on Joshua that "challenges readers to reflect on how conquest shaped America's identity and how it continues to influence American attitudes and actions."²¹ I discuss the relationship between the conquest narrative and America briefly in chapter 1, and *Joshua in 3-D* provides a detailed account for further study, specifically guiding theological reflection on the intertwining of Joshua, the history of violence within the conquest narrative, Christianity, and America. Hawk argues for a realistic look at the violence of conquest saturated throughout the history of the United States but also finds possibility for the future. He asks, "What might happen if America exemplified how a nation can repent and reconcile with the sins of its past?"²² The same question can be asked of the church: "What might happen if the church exemplified how an institution can repent and reconcile with the sins of its past?"

²¹L. Daniel Hawk, *Joshua in 3-D: A Commentary on Biblical Conquest and Manifest Destiny* (Eugene, OR: Cascade, 2010), back cover.

²²Hawk, *Joshua in 3-D*, 257.

Index

133, 140, 149, 151
present-day, 112, 153–54
Coleman, Monica, 150n16
colonialism
    and Christianity, xxi, xxv, 21, 98,
        101, 136–38, 148, 159
    and conquest narrative, xiii–xiv,
        xxvi, 2, 62, 101–2, 104, 138,
        146, 148, 157–59
communitas movements, 47, 69,
    122–23, 140, 149–50, 154
conquest narrative
    Americas, 99–102, 104, 138, 169
    archaeological evidence, xvi–
        xviii, xviin8, xxv, 3, 25, 52, 59,
        72, 111, 160
    Assyria, xxi, 73, 92, 126
    and Christianity, xx, xxiv, xxvi,
        1–3, 22, 98–99, 104, 136, 138,
        162, 169
    and colonialism, xiii–xiv, xxvi, 2,
        62, 101–2, 104, 138, 146, 148,
        157–59
    Europe, 3, 99, 101–2, 136, 158
    and genocide, 79, 93, 127, 140
    historicity of, xvii, 22, 52, 60
    Iron Age, 59–61
    and Israel, xviii, xx, xxviii, 52,
        58–60, 73–75, 77–78, 91–92,
        94, 98, 101n75
    and Judah, xx, 74, 79, 92n55
    as propaganda, 47, 88, 106, 108
    and trauma, xxi, 73n4, 82
    United States, xxix, 1, 3, 105–6,
        161, 169
    and violence, xix, xxviii, 5, 98,
        99n68, 99n69, 101n75, 105,
        151, 156, 169
conquest theory, 58–59, 61–62, 68
Cooke, Bernard J., 7n19
Coote, Robert B., 67, 79n20
counterhistories, xxiv–xxv, 18, 109,
    111–12, 140, 156
countermemories, xxiv, 16, 18, 70,
    111

critical race theory, 5, 106
Cross, Frank Moore, 45, 163n14
Crossan, John Dominic, 18n46
Crumley, Carole, 65n151
Crusades, 99, 103
cultic practices, xvii, 50, 84, 96–97
cults
    archaeological evidence, 26, 36
    Bull Site, 49
    and egalitarianism, 51
    and Josianic reform, 85–88
    serpent, 96
    Yahwist, 44, 50, 84, 95–96
cultural memory
    and Exodus, 24, 56–57, 118, 120,
        124–25
    as interpretive approach, xxviii,
        16n37, 48n96, 55–56, 120, 125

Dallaire, Hélène M., 52, 60–61
David, 74, 84, 87–88, 90, 104
DeMille, Cecil B., 129
DeSantis, Ron, 5
Deuteronomistic History. *See* DH
Deuteronomistic reforms. *See* Josia-
    nic reforms
Deuteronomistic texts
    Assyrian influence, 92
    Deuteronomic Law, 87n40
    and developing ideology, 82–83,
        89, 91, 94–95, 97
    and monotheistic theology, 82
Dever, William G., 24n4, 27n11,
    34n35, 36n45, 36n46, 40n61,
    45–46, 48n96, 49, 67, 68n160,
    72n3, 96n62, 96n63
DH (Deuteronomistic History)
    Assyrian influence, 73, 83n32,
        92, 95, 97n64
    and biblical literacy, 162
    context and development, 75, 80,
        90–91, 94–95, 163–65
    and Exodus, 125
    and Joshua, 60
    and Josiah, 83–84